The Truth about eBay

The Truth about eBay

How to successfully sell part time or full time on eBay

Millions are Doing It—So Can You!

Donny Lowy

Writers Club Press
New York Lincoln Shanghai

The Truth about eBay
How to successfully sell part time or full time on eBay

All Rights Reserved © 2003 by Donny Lowy

Writers Club Press
an imprint of iUniverse, Inc.

For information address:
iUniverse
2021 Pine Lake Road, Suite 100
Lincoln, NE 68512
www.iuniverse.com

ISBN: 0-595-27003-4

Printed in the United States of America

Preface

This publication is designed to provide accurate and authoritative information in regard to the subject matter covered. It is sold with the understanding that the author is not engaged in rendering legal, accounting, financial, investment, or other professional service. If legal advice or other expert assistance is required, the services of a competent professional person should be sought. The information in this book is only for educational purposes and should never be used unless one has first personally consulted with a licensed professional. By reading this book you are acknowledging that you could lose 100% of any money that you might decide to spend. You may read this book for entertainment or educational purposes but you should never use the information without the specific instructions of a professional who knows your personal situation.

Introduction

Everyday, people from all over the world can access millions of items listed on eBay across thousands of categories. Since theirs is an international marketplace, sellers are able to take advantage of a colossal venue, which would otherwise cost thousands of dollars for an individual to open and operate. If you have tried to set up a business, or know someone else who has tried, you appreciate the many facets of the whole apparatus: E-mail, advertising in different venues, bookkeeping, accounts receivable and payable, web site content and hosting, having a popular item or service to market, and keeping it stock, follow up with automated response software, creating a database of customers and mailing lists, not to mention all of the store overhead and payroll...well, the list goes on and on. The expense adds up quickly, but the machine of your business requires at least all of this plus your expertise if you are going to be successful.

Feeling a bit overwhelmed? Well, don't. eBay has created a way for you to have all of the tools you need, and more, at your fingertips twenty-four hours a day. They have made it simple to open your personal cyber-door storefront for the sale of just about anything you can think of. A few restrictions are in place only to protect you as a seller and your buyers from anything that could be offensive or promoted as a scam.

There are many sites on the Internet of which each one declares to have THE best tool kit ever to help you make loads of money on eBay. All of these tool kits sell for a lot of money. How do you think these guys make money? They sell the information many times over, and little else. You will need support from time to time and you deserve to have your questions and problems resolved in a timely manner without getting the run around no matter what time of the day. eBay offers a twenty-four hour a day online tech support that is the best in the online marketplace industry.

Getting excited? Next, let's discuss the motivation of current, successful eBay business people.

Millions of people around the world are sick of their day jobs. They put in many hours, sometimes eighty a week, for little compensation. Getting up early in the morning, driving the rat race, doing a job that they are over qualified is common in this country. The paycheck pays the bills with little money, if any, left over. Few bonuses and pats on the back follow, though certainly deserved. "They (employers) may be thinking that retention (of employees) isn't a viable issue because the economy and the layoffs that go with it make it an employer's market. If employees leave, they reason, that means one fewer worker who has to be laid off," according to a recent interview with the CEO of ITT. The idea that if you are an unhappy company worker in this age of sudden downsizing, you are met with certain apathy. Better, you resign than be fired. Either may be inevitable. The costs in healthcare due to illness caused from employee stress, missed days, and unproductiveness cost employers billions of dollars a year. The media alarms us about recession and the dismal future of getting ahead. Some employer's have their sites set on the bottom line and nothing else.

What's the answer? Going into business for yourself could be the solution. Granted, it is a thought that brings instant excitement, causing the imagination to begin to whirl. The sky is the limit to what you can do. People will always afford items and services they seek no matter what the economy.

Stories abound of people who began with an idea in their garage, building a customer base through the years. They are now rich and have the freedom the rest of us only dream about. Just look at the woman who began Mrs. Fields Cookies. She began in her small kitchen giving out samples on sidewalks. She is now a multi-millionaire.

Lillian Vernon began making purses with her father in their basement. She has had a successful catalog business for decades. Jasmine Jordan, with a love for the publishing industry, launched her magazine, *Tools for Living*, with $300.00 in seed money from her brother. A few years later, she is ready to take her venture to the next level. However, like any enterprising small business owner, she knows her mission: "Make something out of nothing." Jordan's advice is about the best I have ever heard.

The stories are countless of entrepreneurs who have made a good living out of a mere thought, and grew to be very successful.

Creating your own business can fill you with overwhelming feelings. What will you sell? How do you break into eBay? Do you have the equipment: desire, determination, and patience? Do you have the know-how and the energy to constantly learn how to make your business the best it can be? Does this venture take any special talent or education? Will eBay give me the full support a new business needs to get off the ground? How will I be able to handle payments, orders, complaints, and queries?

This book will give you the answers. Herein are the answers and support you need to begin an entirely new lifestyle. *The eBay Business Guide* is not a get rich quick scheme, and the money is not going to begin to flow in by next Saturday. It is, however, a book that is filled with the no-nonsense information, tips and advice that will help you get into eBay with ease. No book can give you the determination you will need to be successful. That is up to you.

What is your ideal lifestyle? Is it to have enough money to pay your bills as they come in, have some extra money to buy what you want, and do what you love to do? Would you like to work out of your own home, be your own boss, dress down not only on Fridays but every day? Do you have youngsters in your home who need help with college expenses? Is your heart's desire to quit your low paying, stressful job and make eBay your only income? It can be done!

Not having sufficient time for family is the number one complaint of the work force today. Enough time and money is not just a pipe dream that plays repeatedly in your mind on a daily basis. It can be your dream come true! Millions are doing it. Why not you?

Yes, you will come up against hurdles and seemingly impenetrable barriers. You will get tired, frustrated and discouraged. Problems go with the territory. You must have an attitude that problems are only a temporary challenge, and you have the smarts to get through them. Challenges make us stronger. Obstacles are mere trials that bring an entrepreneur to the front of the battlefield in order to do what it takes to succeed, to achieve their deepest dreams and desires. Without these hurdles, we would be bored and learn very little.

> **"Go confidently in the direction of your dreams. Live the life you have imagined."** —*Henry David Thoreau*

Look at your new business venture as a learning process. Know in your heart and mind that, <u>yes</u>, you can do this, and you <u>**will**</u> achieve what you set out to accomplish. Lose the word "if" from your vocabulary! Confidence in your abilities is not a gift. It cannot be bought. Confidence in yourself comes from a mental process in which you <u>constantly</u> chase the doubts out, and replace them with positive declarations. It's hard work until you finally believe yourself.

Negative input from friends and family will no doubt make you wonder if you are doing the right thing. Only one person knows—you. Do not incorporate into your thinking or feelings what the nay sayers will inevitably have to say about your business ideas. They will always be there for you with a good dose of negativity, especially when you get discouraged. I could never understand pessimists. Maybe they like everyone else to be as miserable as they are. I just smile, let them have their say, and then become ever more motivated to make my idea work. The only people you have to account to are yourself and your immediate family.

So get mentally charged! Look in the mirror every day and tell yourself, *"I can do this!"*

> *"A great deal of talent is lost to the world for want of a little courage. Every day sends to their graves obscure men whose timidity prevented them from making a first effort." —Sydney Smith*

The fact that you're interested in learning more about making money by selling on eBay shows that you're ready to take the next step that most people never get to. You want to learn how to take responsibility for yourself and not rely on someone else.

Well you'll be pleased to know that **it's easy**! If you can use a computer to get this far, you can use it to **make money.**

Once you get going, the thrill of watching bids mount up on your auctions, and getting checks in the mail every day, will make you want to develop your business further.

Join the hundreds of others who are supplementing their income, or replacing it, with money made from eBay auctions. The best thing of all is that it's all done from the comfort of your home!

What Can eBay Do For You?

It is something more than going to a mega chain, where you can buy anything under one roof. eBay provides a selling and buying atmosphere in the comfort of your home, or wherever you may be. eBay brings everything to you. Moreover, more and more people are catching on to the shop from home idea. Before the Internet, catalog shopping enjoyed overwhelming growth as a multi-billion dollar a year industry. Now, the Internet, especially eBay, has provided the most convenient selling and buying atmosphere one could ever find

If a seller has business integrity and cares for each and every one of his/her customers, that honesty will shine through because of eBay's great customer service abilities that are available to sellers. Business decency is what will keep your customers coming back, giving you the reputation that customers can count on. When you shop in the outside world, do you continue giving your hard earned cash to those stores who have not provided you with the utmost in customer care? Of course not. So, it is with your eBay business. What keep customers coming back repeatedly are the customer satisfaction, seller integrity and convenience.

eBay provides you with an instant worldwide market! Imagine what you would have to go through in time and cost in order to gain access to such a phenomenal amount of potential customers. The same amount of customer access in a real world business would take many years to accumulate. eBay has put your customer base at your fingertips!

Many folks have started out on eBay as a hobby, bringing a few extra bucks to the household. They have found that with a little more effort and commitment, those few bucks have turned into a major family business. They are now allowed the freedom they only dreamed of previously. What could be better than turning a hobby, something you enjoy doing, into a full fledged, profitable venture?

This is not a get rich quick scheme. It will take patience and perseverance to set up your eBay store or auction. Nevertheless, it will be yours; the baby you grew from nothing to something you can brag about—a real money making business with your name on it.

Once you get started, it only takes a **few hours** of work each week to place your listings on the eBay or Amazon auction sites and then you can watch the bids roll in!

It's hard to believe that something so simple can work so well! In fact, it is so easy that you might make the choice hundreds of others have—and **fire**

your boss!! As soon as you see the checks coming into your mailbox, you'll realize that **you can** do it!

There is a harsh reality to going into business, and you need to know about it. There are **TWO Business Worlds** out there.

1.) The **Dreamer's Business World**

2.) The **REAL Business World**

If you really want to make money on the Internet, you're going to have to put down the Teddy Bear and pack away the jammies, and the fluff. You must leave Never-Never Land, and enter the Real Business World.

What I have said above about having confidence and not allowing others to sway you from your dreams is true. However, you must also go into your venture with your eyes wide open so as not to get scammed, waste money and eventually fail. You have to learn a balance of excitement for the possibilities, and good old-fashioned logic and common sense. It's too bad that many folks greedily take advantage of our trust and honesty for their own means to an end. Nevertheless, that's the way it is in this world. Don't let it discourage or anger you. Just keep your goals in mind and move ahead. If a piece of advice or information doesn't move you **FOR-WARD**, forget it.

Let's compare:

In the **Dreamer's Business World:**

- All you have to do is make a few "Easily Affordable Payments," and your Internet Store will magically appear with virtually no effort on your part.

- **Your Personal Business Mentor** will leap out of bed in the middle of the night and come racing to your side every time you have the slightest question.

- Tinkerbell the Fairy will dance out across the globe and gently waft millions of customers to your web site on fluffy clouds of cash.

- Everybody on Earth only wants to buy one kind of product: cheap, imported, off-brand Junk.

- You will **always be able to offer the best prices** on Earth for anything you sell online, and nobody will be able to beat you in competition.

That's the Dreamer's Business World. Wouldn't it be great if the Dreamers Business World were a fact? We could all live peacefully in harmony, minding our own business. However, the only fact of it is—this kind of thinking will make you fail.

Now let's talk about the Real Business World.

In the **Real Business World:**

- Get-Rich-Quick Schemes **do not work. PERIOD.**

- If something **seems** to good to be true, it **IS** too good to be true.

- Don't expect anyone to hold your hand or wipe your brow for you. The only person you need to have expectations from is you. That's the favorite method of the Scam Artist. While he's holding your hand and wiping your brow, he's lifting your wallet. **Be prepared to WORK and LEARN.**

- If you're in a **big hurry to make a lot of money,** you should **not** be starting a business. You should be searching your family tree for an old, rich relative to be VERY nice to.

The Real Business World is not for wimps. It involves **work, persistence, patience,** and an ability to **listen & learn.** It's not a place where you can stamp your feet and yell, "Hey, no fair!" or "If you don't stop that, I'm not going to play anymore!" Nasty, unreasonable customers are a fact in the business world. Learn how to be diplomatic and how to resolve problems in a reasonable but firm manner without letting it get to you

I have had my own business since 1995. I learned early on that clients can be difficult. With a firm, but fair, business policy in place, there is no reason for irresolvable problems. Every retail store has a store policy, which stems the customer problems that might crop up. Be fair when you do this; think how you like to be treated when you are the customer.

There will be bumps in the road. If you're not willing to ride them out, you shouldn't bother getting started in the first place.

However, the rewards you reap in the **Real Business World** are **more than equal** to the work you put in. **This is how REALLY successful people actually BECOME successful!**

Everybody who starts out in business wants to succeed. Some already know what needs to be done. However, there are a large number of people who either have the wrong ideas from the start, or they've been fed the wrong ideas over time (from watching too many infomercials). The previously mentioned information scammers will tell you that bundles of cash is waiting for you tomorrow, if only you will buy their book or tape.

Then of course, there are those **few** who are just plain lazy, and want something for nothing.

Here's a quick recap of this section:

- For those who **don't want to do the work** to **really** succeed, a Get-Rich-Quick Infomercial is only as far away as your TV Remote Control. Sweet Dreams.

- If someone tells you they'll hold your hand throughout your whole business start-up, make sure your OTHER hand has a tight grip on your wallet.

- Don't expect to make a lot of money overnight, ANYWHERE! **Real success** takes time, and a solid foundation to build on. Walk before you run!

- Be willing to **listen and learn!** There IS good information out here. You'll be able to tell what's good, and what's TOO good to be true.

- **Treat people with respect!** You never know when you might be emailing someone who could give you your next big break! Network with other entrepreneurs.

- **Keep your confidence high!** Bah to the negative and the pessimists.

The Real Business World is the most exciting place you'll ever go. Watching your business begin to grow and become successful is an absolute thrill ride, equal to none I've ever experienced. It's **worth the work**, every minute of it. Don't let the Scam Artists cheat you out of that.

The idea is to choose a service or item(s) that people want, set up a store, auction or both that is pleasing to the eye and will bring in business, and then fill orders. This venture is supposed to be something you love to do. That is the secret to a successful eBay business. Loving what you do is most of the battle when it comes to making money. If you don't, you won't have the determination it takes to succeed. You will become bored and soon liken your new business to that old job you had out in the workforce. The problem with the work force today is that very few employees enjoy their job. Hence, apathy sets in along with dissatisfaction that causes discouragement and depression. *Do what you love.* This key will provide you with the greatest amount of satisfaction and the greatest feeling of accomplishment **you will ever have!**

YOUR eBAY STRATEGY

The key to making enormous profits on eBay is to develop an efficient strategy long before you list your first item. You need to know what types of products you want to sell, where to find your niche market at eBay, and develop a profile of your average customer.

There are two types of sellers on eBay, which I call **High Volume Listers** and **Low Volume Listers**. High Volume Listers re those who list more and keep more than 10 auctions online at a time. Low Volume Listers are those whole list fewer than 10 auctions at a time.

The profit margin of the product you sell determines which category you will fit into.

For example, if you sell real estate and make $10,000 per sale, you may only need to list a few properties each week on eBay to make a real killing with you Internet business. The same applies for the sale of expensive jewelry, autos, and other items that fit into this category. However, if you sell magazines, for example, you will make only $5 to $10 per sale. In that case, you need to list hundreds of items to make a large profit. This would make you a High Volume Seller. So why would you list hundreds of items when it seems easier to list a few large items and make a fortune?

The answer lies in this one truth: ONLINE BUYERS ARE MOST WILLING TO PSEND UNDER $50.00 FOR A PRODUCT. This makes sense—would you pay thousands for something you have never seen? Another reason High Volume Listers are more common is because it is much easier and profitable to buy inexpensive items at wholesale prices, but very difficult to buy real estate or vehicles at wholesale prices.

With this information, you must consider the product you are selling and an informed decision as to whether you want to be a High or Low Volume seller. Your decision will depend on how much you have to spend on your new entrepreneurial business. If you have only have a few hours in the evenings and weekends, you might choose the Low Volume option until your business really takes off. But, if you are making the big leap to a full time income, you would likely choose the High Volume option. Do you want to start out slow, or go for it full time right off? Only you can choose which way to begin, as you are in control of how much time you have.

You will need to project your goals to the future. To what degree do you want to your business to grow? Take a look at this scenario:

You have identified your niche. You have decided, for example, that you want to sell jewelry. You have found the associated categories. You have found that buyers will typically spend from $50.00 to $100.00 per purchase and your auction profits will be about $60.00. You have plenty of time and your profit margin is low, so you decide to become a High Volume Seller on eBay and you will list 100–200 auctions per week. The average number of winning bids will be around 70%, which is the average on eBay. Your calculated weekly income will be in the neighborhood of $6300. You have set up an account with a jewelry wholesaler and have already purchased enough inventory to cover your first week. **Plan on re-listing your auctions as soon as they end.** Don't waste time! If you are getting sales soon after listing, get more merchandise back up.

In the example above, notice that the seller thought of everything before listing a single item, making sure that he/she was prepared for the task ahead and establishing a solid game=plan. It is vital that you project your sales into the future, think of any possible problems that may come up, and resolve them before they happen.

KNOW YOUR SALES STRATEGY BEFORE YOU START!

For the next several weeks, you need to pay close attention to what is selling, the price your items are going for, and their popularity. Write it all down and keep careful records. If you go into selling on eBay haphazardly, it's going to show in your profit margin and overall success.

YOUR AUCTION IS OVER...

Now what do you do? You are pretty excited that you have made your first sale. Now you know that this can really be done. Congratulations! Now you send an e-mail to the buyer to let them know that they won, and give them any special instructions they may need. You tell them how the item is going to be shipped, the extra cost for shipping and handling. Let them know that the item will be shipped as soon as you receive payment. This will help the buyer to feel more confident and will help your payment to arrive in a timely manner. Good communication is necessary, especially for first time buyers. Don't forget to thank the buyer for their bid. If there will be a delay in shipping the item, let the buyer know. This is only good business.

Give the buyer some good comments on their feedback form. This helps buyers to be able to create confidence with other sellers. Hopefully, they will do the same for you, which will help you create a good business practice reputation.

Should the bidder back out on you, there is not a lot you can do about it. There are always emergencies that can come up, so don't give up on them right away. If it does seem as though the bidder is not going to pay, leave a negative feedback on them. If you have to list that item again, you can probably do it free. eBay has a policy that protects sellers should buyers back out.

The First Step

The first step is to acquire the right information. The unfortunate truth is that there is a lot of nonsense information being sold on the web. It fills people with false hope then leads them down a dead end path. Let me give you a quick way to separate the trash from the truth:

ANY SYSTEM FOR MAKING MONEY ON THE INTERNET, WHICH DOESN'T EXPLAIN A FEW BASIC PRINCIPLES, IS A SCAM.

As with any other moneymaking idea, too many people are willing to sell you very little information for too much money. That is how they make their income; selling useless information. Both television (infomercials) and the Internet abound with people who make their big money selling phony information. You have to be careful to weed out the scam artists in order to get to the honest information providers whose only motivation is to **teach you what you need to know in order to be successful.**

The eBay site has an excellent support system for their registered users. They want you to be successful so that they, too, will continue to enjoy success.

Founded in September 1995, eBay is the leading marketplace for online sale of goods and services by a diverse community of businesses and individuals like you. If measured by total user minutes and clicks, according to Media Metrix, eBay is the most popular shopping site on the Internet, boasting over 49.7 million registered users and 39 billion clicks a month. By the time you are finished reading this informative book, you will be ready to join their vast membership and be able to access the state of the art selling tools that only eBay can offer.

eBay's mission is to help practically anyone trade practically anything on earth.

eBay enables trade on a local, national and international basis. They feature a variety of international sites, specialty sites, categories and services that provide users with all of the necessary tools for efficient and profitable online trading in the auction-style and fixed price formats.

In 2000, the eBay community transacted more than $5 billion in annualized gross merchandise sales (value of goods traded on the eBay site).

I know of no other site on the Internet who has everything one could need to be successful. Just recently, eBay reaffirmed its financial goals for 2003 and its 2005 revenue goal of $3 billion. At the end of their third quarter, there were 24.2 million unique users on eBay and $511 billion in gross merchandise sales per active user. How can you, as a potential seller of goods and services lose? You will be a winner by <u>learning, growing and working hard.</u>

Now that you know that eBay can lead you to the success of your dreams, let's get down to the tools that will help you to achieve your goals!

Business Plan

The first truth is that you are indeed an entrepreneur! An entrepreneur is a person who organizes, operates and assumes the risk of a business. Operating an eBay venture out of your home makes you no less of a bonafide business owner! You will still have to decide on what to sell, how to advertise it so you get interest, keep records of sales, fees and customer input, do your bookkeeping, etc. Isn't all of that what a business owner has to do? The "home cottage business" has been growing by leaps and bounds for the last ten years.

A business plan is a written model for what you wish to achieve with your new business. This is where you write down your goals and a systematic plan on how to get there. A well-thought business plan is an essential must-do for startup ventures. It'll be required for any credit or other financing, but even if you're flying solo on a shoestring, a business plan will help keep you focused on what you know will create success. You will need to refer to it often to keep your goals in sight. In the Appendix Section are web sites where you can get samples and help on how to write up your own personal business plan.

Your visitors come to your site to get something that will benefit them, and they're more likely to need additional information with which to justify the purchase than would a consumer.

Provide your visitor the information they need to make a decision, plus materials that will help them sell the idea to those who sign the check. Give the visitor what they need to convince others that buying from you is a good idea. How? By explaining the benefits of your product more than talking about your company.

To start tuning your strategy, you don't have to change anything about what you are doing right now. Just begin to refine the way you communicate with your business visitor by trimming out the fat. How do you know what to trim? Contact and survey your customers — ask what they would like to see on your site, and what they like about your site. Then contact members of your target audience, and develop a profile of what they want, need, and expect from the type of site you provide. Shape your implementation around the purpose of your site, considering each different method as it supports your business objectives.

These strategies will get you started on the path to successfully serving a business-to-business market. Remember, you don't have to provide everything on your Website — just those things that support the purpose of your site. If you must, publish other content on other people's sites, but don't clutter your site with things that distract your visitor from their requirements and your site's objectives. It will only frustrate the business visitor and harm the relationship you're trying to establish.

The worst mistake you can make in setting up your eBay business is to minimize the idea that you are, indeed, a businessperson. You make be selling items you love, and you may be enjoying your new entrepreneurship, and that is what you are supposed to get out of this. But you must plan and use success strategies to be successful.

What To Sell?

You might want to fill your online store with round tuits, or an amazing sponge that never dries up, but who will want to buy a constantly soaked sponge?

You have to have a marketable product. Note the keyword *marketable.*

This killer gets most businesses. They might have everything else right, but starting without a high demand product is a surefire way to fail fast. Most people get caught up in the whirlwind of selling a product without ever stopping to ask: "Does anyone want what I'm selling?"

To be successful on the web, you have to start right, by picking products that already have a market. You need to know what types of products are proven sellers. Then find out if your product is right for sure by testing that demand without spending much money. This way you'll know from the very beginning whether your product will be a success without starting to work seriously yet.

Choosing Your Products

Too many people make the mistake of trying to sell only products that they, themselves, like. Others make the mistake of trying to sell only the coolest and flashiest things they can find.

Buying and selling is not new. People have been doing it since the beginning of time in one form or another. Everyone wants or needs things that they, themselves, cannot provide. So we go to people who can provide what we want. In turn, we pay those people for the products or services we want.

Deciding what to sell is not as easy as it looks. There are two main types of items that people will be selling. The first are those items that are lying around your house that you no longer need, like those CD's you no longer listen to, old toys from your childhood, nick knacks, things that are junk to you but could well be a treasure for someone else. Such items are great to sell to make some extra money, but they are a one-time sale. Once they are sold, they are gone as is your chance of recurring income.

The second category of items that you can sell is products that you create or buy and resell them. These can be a wonderful source of extra income, things as simple as your grandmother's chocolate chip cookie recipe or any other recipe, a disk or book about Beanie Babies, hand-crafted items, collectors items, antiques, etc. These things can be sold repeatedly. They may not bring in as much of an income as you desire, but you can sell them in great quantities. There are no limits to what you can sell to put some fast cash into your pocketbook. Is it more than just "fast cash" that you want? Read on for other ideas that will take you into a bigger, more profitable business.

Items That You Can Sell in Quantity

There are many types of items that you can sell in quantity. You would purchase these things in quantity in order to sell. Collectibles that are very popular, but not available worldwide, such as sports figurines (the sports industry is a multi-billion dollar a year market), dolls, trading cards, beanie babies, teddy bears, jewelry, etc. You can buy and sell virtually anything at a modest profit and it is fair game as long you remember that people on eBay demand low prices. It is better to sell 100 reports for $5.00 than 20 for $10.00.

There is no limit to the type of things that you can auction off. By doing a search on eBay, you will find people are selling everything from toys, computers, photography equipment, books, clothing, antiques, even homes and vehicles! Your choices are unlimited.

How do you decide what to sell? First, make up a list of the items that you are considering. Your list should include items that you enjoy making such as craft items. The craft industry is a huge market. Most people love handcrafted things, but don't want the bother it takes to make them. Plus they love the look of something that is one of a kind. Be very specific with your list. Write down the description of the item, what you paid for it, or the cost of materials and time you put into making it. The smallest details mean a higher price.

Now, take your list and do a search on eBay for the types of items you have on your list. Research if there are items similar to yours and what they sell for. This will give you a good idea of the market for your item, as well as a good idea of customer interest. When doing your search choose keywords. If you are looking for Beanie Babies, just type that in. If you are looking for Alan Jackson's Greatest Hits, type in Alan Jackson. You will be amazed at the number of items and categories eBay offers.

Once you find the same categories and the same types of items you want to sell, you will learn a few different things. First, you will see how popular your item is at eBay. You can get a good idea on what the market price is. You will also learn if the market for your item is already too common to add to. You will also see what you can expect to get for your item or service, and how many people are expressing interest by the auction activity. Obviously, if you have fifty different people bidding on an item, it's a lot more apt to bring in money than an item that is being bid on by only a few people. Of course, this is not a rule cemented in stone. All you need is one bid to sell your item or service. After you do all of this research, you can now set out with an idea of what you should bring in for selling your items.

Don't worry if you find others selling the same items that you want to sell. It doesn't mean the market is already full. People like to have choices. If you see that someone else is successful selling your same idea, then that means you can be successful too! For example, I looked up "cigars" on eBay. While I found 412 items in that category, half of them were just cigar related like pictures of people holding cigars, figurines, etc. Four hundred twelve items in one category is a very small classification. Your chances would be better than average should you want to sell all kinds of cigars from perhaps a wholesaler. We will talk about wholesaling later.

HOT ITEMS

One of the most recent fads are the Spice Girls dolls. Stores couldn't keep them on the shelves, and people are willing to pay a premium price for them. Time is very valuable to your buyers. They would rather not drive to every Wal-Mart, K-Mart, etc. hoping to find the one thing they want most. They would much rather sit at their desk, log on to eBay, type in a few keywords, and pay a little more to get that special item.

CREATE & PRODUCE ITEMS THAT YOU CAN SELL YOURSELF

Are you expert on something? Can you make doll clothes that aren't available in stores, and can you make them cheaper? There aren't a lot of choices for doll clothes out there. Can you fix computers? Write a book about it. Look at all the books for "dummies." They sell like chili on a cold day. Do you love to make handcrafted items? You might have one of a kind patterns. Market them! Can you write short booklets filled with good information? Do you have a knack for finding unusual fishing gear? Toot your horn as the expert in whatever you like to do or make and sell it.

We aren't trying to reinvent the wheel here, nor are we trying to be a nuclear physicist. You are just trying to take a simple idea, nurture it, and build it into a business that will not only bring you extra income but great satisfaction as well. Over 30,000 people have made selling on eBay their main, and sometimes only, income. Remember Mrs. Fields? She began

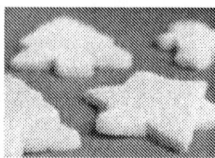

with *cookies.*

So use your imagination, examine your unique talents and look at what products are in demand. The Beanie Baby craze won't last forever. Imagine if you were the person to think that up. The simplest ideas are the ones that change your life.

You need to keep in mind that people will buy virtually anything as long as you are offering an item that is quality and sold at a fair price.

The best place to start thinking about a sellable item is to look to what you like to do. Do you have a hobby that could turn into a profitable item? Below is a list of possible ideas. Of course, this is only a partial list. Your own ideas are only limited to what you can imagine. eBay itself will give you an exhaustive list of what people are doing.

⇒ **Woodworking**: the craft business is a billion dollar a year industry. Craftsmen and artisans paint wood figures and shapes to sell. Quality woodworking is always in demand.

⇒ **Jewelry**: do you have a talent for making beautiful and unusual jewelry? This is also a many billion dollar a year industry.

⇒ **Crafts**: do you make unusual craft items like custom photograph albums, whirligigs, wall hangings, clocks, quilts or afghans?

⇒ **Event Planner Services**: Weddings, Anniversaries, Birthdays, Bar Mitzvahs, etc.

⇒ **Authors**: sell your books on eBay without the hassle. Folks are always looking for information.

⇒ **Wholesale buying**: there are many wholesalers who sell every kind of item from A to Z. Catalogs are easy to get.

⇒ **Drop Shipping**: there is a fantastic way to get access to in demand products without having to stock a single item. It's called drop shipping. This where a vendor (you) takes orders online, gets the payment, then forwards the order on to the distributor who ships out the product as if it came directly from the vendor.

Most businesses selling tangible products on the web are using drop-shipping companies to supply the products & fulfill the orders. **Through drop shipping, you can start a business with literally no money.** We will talk more about that later.

⇒ **Sports Cards and Memorabilia:** sports of all kinds are enjoying the greatest support in history.

⇒ **Antiques:** dealer authentic, or nick knacks from local stores

⇒ **Toys:** vintage or new. Perhaps you make original teddy bears or other items for children.

⇒ **NASCAR** memorabilia

⇒ **Cook books and recipes**

⇒ **Coins, Comics, Historical items**

⇒ **Dolls and clothes:** vintage to Barbie and baby dolls

⇒ **Custom Photo Frames and Photography**

⇒ **Needlecraft and Pottery**

⇒ **Autos:** there is a special category for vehicles.

⇒ **Health and Beauty Products:** these are very inexpensive when bought through wholesale dealers.

⇒ **Coins**

⇒ **Computers and accessories**

⇒ **Holiday Items**—every holiday from Christmas to Valentines to Thanksgiving

⇒ **Cash cards and phone cards**

⇒ **Specialty or Imported Cigar and Tobacco related products.**

You can see that the list is endless. Find your niche. The most important thing you can do is to visit the eBay site and look around for the items that people are seeking, and what is selling best. With your own niche, however, you can create a market. With the right advertising, your niche can be a hot selling category.

eBay's community has as many discussion boards as there are categories of items for sale. If you have a problem with sales, ads, customer service, buyers, or anything else, just click on communities and find your answer. Other sellers have come up against the same obstacles you might have, and they will have the answer. There are also chat rooms to talk to other sellers for tips or just for fun and sharing. The 'hot items list" is available at http://forums.ebay.com/dws?14@1034353879994@.ef74be0

Creating A Winning Ad

Now that you've surfed through eBay to check out who is selling what, prices and what other's ads look like. It can be frustrating and overwhelming at first because there's so many selling sites to sift through. It's like looking through the classifieds except that you have to click on the titles to see the rest of the ads. It is a virtual maze as you try to weed out the exact items that you are looking for. You will feel like you are in an information overload. But your job as a seller is to cut through the tangle and get your ad viewed by as many people as you possibly can so that they can find you.

In order for someone to see your ad, they have to have their curiosity piqued, place their mouse over your ad and click. If your ad is common and like everyone else's you aren't going to stand out. Therefore, no matter how good your item and price is, they aren't going to see it. So, your ads are extremely important. They must stand out above all the rest.

Use Applicable Words In Your Title

You would be surprised at how many ads tell you absolutely nothing. You must be very specific in your titles about what you are selling. If you are selling an antique clock, don't just put "CLOCK." That doesn't tell your prospective buyer anything. There are millions of clocks and buyers look for specifics. Your clock may be in the clock section on eBay, but it won't get noticed. Use something like "RARE Antique 1863 Clock." You will be amazed at how many more clicks you will receive.

Remember that prospective buyers will use the search feature to find what they want to buy. So you have to make sure you include the words that they are looking for. If someone collects sports cards, they will type in a specific player in the search. If your ad says, "Sports Cards," they will likely miss your 1995 Michael Jordan rare. If you are selling something with a specific paint scheme, put that in your ad. In short, think about what your buyer is searching for and give it to them in the title of your ad.

Use The Right Words

You want to use words that will grab the attention of the buyer. Because they have literally thousands and thousands of titles to look at, you want them to notice yours. How will you be able to get their attention?

For a small fee of about $2.00, you can get your title listed in bold face. While that helps to get your ad noticed, it is not the best way. You must learn how to use **POWER WORDS**.

Power words are words that lend a sense of urgency to your ad. Descriptors such as **RARE, UNLIMITED, STUNNING, UNBELIEVABLE, ONE OF A KIND** will get your buyer to notice you.

Look at these two titles:

NASCAR Die-cast Models

"RARE DALE EARNHARDT RED AND WHITE DIECAST"

Which one gets your attention? Probably most of you said the second one. Using all capital letters is a great way to make your items stand out, but it can be overkill. Take a look at the next one.

"RARE **DALE EARNHARDT** Red and White **DIECAST** Awesome!"

Your brain tends to pick up on the different fonts first. It also looks more professional without the overkill. The buyer sees what is most important right in the title. Regardless how you use bold and capitals, you want your title to stand out from the rest.

You need to keep records to keep track of which kind of titles has created the most attention. Try a few different things to see which works best. From your records, you will be able to keep track of which titles and ads work the best.

To recap: when it comes to the title, be descriptive, use exciting attention grabbing words and set your ad apart from the others!

WRITING DESCRIPTIONS THAT SELL!

Now that you've gotten buyers to look at your ad, you want them to bid on your item. Your item must be as appealing as possible, motivating buyers to bid right away. If buyers leave without placing a bid, it is likely they will not be back.

Be Specific

The overall description of your item is of utmost importance. Do not leave any room for confusion or speculation of what is for sale. Write the most graphic and specific description you can. If there is anything unique about your item, say it. If there are any flaws be sure to write that in too. List any special features. Always remember: if people do not feel comfortable bidding on something they are not sure of, you won't make a sale. If there are any dents or flaws at all in your item, you must disclose it. This is to protect yourself from problems down the road. Buyers are able to give you a kind of report card on your selling integrity. If you have negatives, buyers can read that even before they consider a bid or the outright buying of your item in your store. Obviously, they will pass you up because of your negatives. They expect complete honesty from sellers. I've seen thousands of sellers with not one negative on their record and they have made eBay their main or only source of income. They also have virtually no returns. Below is an example of a description, except I would add something more creative like, "Candy and Cody Christmas Bears are looking for a good home that will love them throughout the whole year." Notice the measurements are also listed.

Description

These sleepy bears will brighten your holiday season. They each play 1 of 3 holiday tunes when you press their paw. Features "We Wish You A Merry Christmas", "Jingle Bells", and "Santa Claus Is Coming To Town." Each bear measures 10 1/2"H.

Use Photographs!

People appreciate and are more confident in buying something they can actually see. Write your ad without the photo so that the picture will stand alone to reinforce your description. In other words, do not rely totally on your photo. Make sure the photo is of good quality. This will show you are a professional and you take great pride in what you sell. A disposable camera will do. You can have the photos put on a disk for a nominal charge, and then put them on your computer in a file for easy access. You can increase your selling power by over 200% by using photos.

A picture gives the buyer a strong visual image of what you are offering. Having the ability to see what is being sold leaves the buyer with that image that will stick in their mind unlike just a description. Search the items on eBay that have photos as opposed to those that don't. You will see that the photographed items sell better with higher bids or selling prices in the stores.

SEEING IS BELIEVING!

Now that you have photos of your items, how do you get them on eBay?

You can do it the normal way and take a picture with just a disposable camera, have it developed at Wal-Mart or other inexpensive photo processor, then scan it into a file on your computer. Or you can go to somewhere like Kinko's and have them put your photos on a disk.

You can also use a digital camera if you have one, which will put the picture directly into a file on your computer. In addition, a camcorder will work with a device like SNAPPY and do it that way.

To make your photos look custom and really stand out, use programs like Photo Shop Pro or Adobe PhotoShop. You can adjust the contrast, color and size of the pictures. These programs also enable you to put fancy text on your photos, make frames around them and many other eye-pleasing effects. The better and more professional your pictures look, the more traffic and buys you will have. I've seen pictures on some seller's sites that are blurred or so small you can't see the item clearly. Which ad do you think is most likely to bring in sales?

How to Add a Photo to Your Listing

Step 1: Copy Your Photo to the Web

There are two ways to get your picture onto the Web so you can include it in your eBay listing:

1. **Use eBay Picture Services.** When you use eBay Picture Services, eBay keeps and displays your pictures for the length of your listing. You'll also be offered enhanced options just for eBay Picture Services users, such as a picture slideshow and Super sized pictures. Storing one picture with no enhancements is free with eBay Picture Services. Additional pictures and features have associated fees.

2. **Host your picture elsewhere.** Perhaps your Internet Service Provider (ISP) gives you some space on the Web where you can store your pictures. Or maybe you'd like to try out picture-hosting services like Pongo, Twaze, or PixHost. The Sell Your Item form has a field where you can enter the Web address (URL) of a picture stored on the Web. That picture will be displayed in your listing. To display more than one externally hosted picture on eBay, you'll have to use HTML in your listing.

1. File transfer software, such as WS_FTP for PCs (includes eBay user reference guide) or Fetch Softworks for Macs will assist in uploading your picture file to your ISP or hosting service.

Add pictures on the Sell Your Item Form

In the section of the Sell Your Item Form labeled Add Pictures, you are given a choice between eBay Picture Services and Web Hosting.

For Web Hosting

Click on the Web Hosting link to enter the Web address of your hosted picture. This Web address (or URL) will look something like this: http://www.host.com/yourfolder/photo.jpg. You can test the address by typing it into a separate window of your browser. If your picture appears, it works! If not, double-check the address.

If you're using Web Hosting, you're done with this tutorial. Happy selling!

For eBay Picture Services
eBay Picture Services is easy to use. It's a bit different depending on your browser and computer platform, however.

Macintosh users with any browser: You need to use Basic eBay Picture Services, which will allow you to upload pictures to eBay, but does not offer more advanced functions.

1. Click on the Basic eBay Picture Services link in the right column of the Sell Your Item Form.

2. To add a picture using Basic eBay Picture Services, click the **Browse** button and locate your file on your hard drive.

Windows users: Look for your browser below to get just the right directions for you.

Internet Explorer 4.0+:
Enhanced eBay Picture Services will let you drag and drop pictures right from a folder on your hard drive onto the Sell Your Item form. It will also let you crop and rotate your pictures right from the selling form.

Here's how to get started:

1. The first time you use Enhanced eBay Picture Services (which is automatically selected in the Sell Your Item form) you'll be prompted to download a small piece of software that will add eBay Picture Services functionality to your computer. You'll see a box like this:

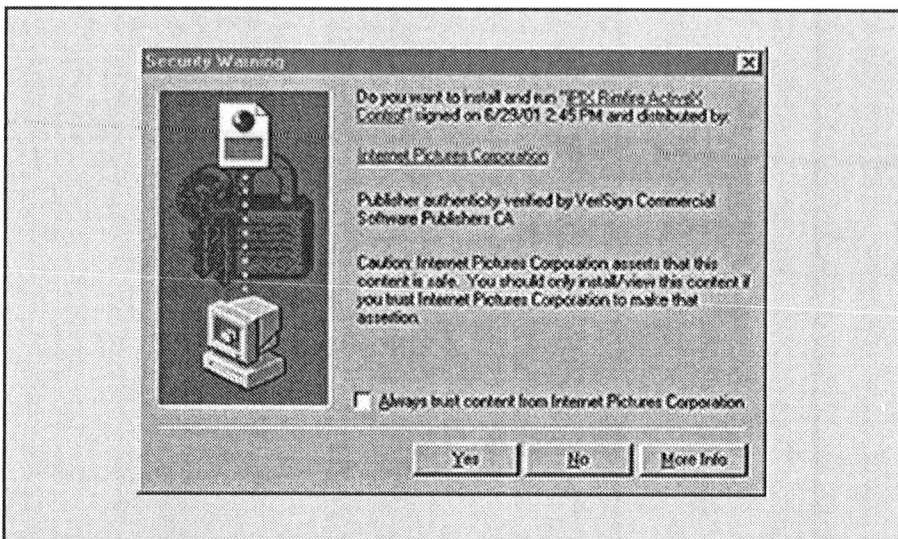

Click Yes to start using the enhanced features. The download will take about one minute.

2.   To add your pictures to eBay Picture Services, click on Add Picture and locate your picture file on your hard drive, then click on Open.

Follow the instructions on the Sell Your Item form to crop and rotate your picture to help it **Netscape Navigator 6.x:** You need to use Basic eBay Picture Services, which will allow you to upload pictures to eBay, but does not offer more advanced functions.

1.   Click on the Basic eBay Picture Services link in the right column of the Sell Your Item form.

2.   To add a picture using Basic eBay Picture Services, click on the Browse button and locate your file on your hard drive.

Now your picture is on the Web and ready to help your items sell!

Make sure your photo looks its best in your listing.

If you need more help go to http://pages.ebay.com/help/sell/photo_tutorial3.html

> Here are some tips **from experienced eBay sellers** for taking photos that will make your item look its best and buyers confidence!

- Use **proper lighting**. Many people find natural, outdoor lighting best. Indoors or out, light your item thoroughly.

- Consider a **backdrop**. If appropriate, consider using a plain, colored fabric backdrop to make your item stand out. Don't use pure white, as it tends to create too much contrast in your photo. If you don't use a backdrop, be sure to move other things out of the way so your item will really stand out.

- Get **close up**! Buyers want to see detail, so really make your item take up the whole frame. Consider taking a close-up of a section of the item in addition to the entire object in order to give buyers a better idea of the item's actual condition.

Edit Your Photo

Once your photo is on your computer hard drive, you can often improve it with photo editing software, which may have come with your digital camera or scanner. You can also download basic editing software from sites like Tucows and Shareware.com.

Tips:

- Remove unnecessary background.
- Balance the contrast and brightness.
- Save your edited picture as a JPEG(.jpg) file (file types other than JPEG and GIF should not be used). Here's how (in most programs):

1.   Choose Save As from the File menu.

2.   Name your file.

3.   Select JPEG (.jpg) or GIF (.gif) from the Save as Type drop-down list.

4.   Planning on hosting your own picture? File size should be under 50 KB (kilobytes) for quick page downloads.

Note: Selecting JPEG or GIF will automatically end your filename with ".jpg" (for example, *carphoto* will now be *carphoto.jpg*).

When you use eBay Picture Services, you can choose to add these enhancements to your listing:

• <u>Title bar picture</u>

• <u>Slide show</u>

• <u>Supersize</u> your picture

• <u>Picture pack</u>: A combination that saves you money

Title Bar Picture
Feature your picture at the top of your listing

• Lets bidders **see your item immediately**—without scrolling

• Uses the first picture you enter in your listing—sizes it automatically

• **Included automatically** with eBay Picture Services

• FREE—available exclusively to **eBay Picture Services users**

Slide Show
Brings your item to life for buyers

- **Automatically creates slide shows** from your pictures (Requires two or more pictures)

- Feature multiple item views to create an "animated effect"

- **Interactive**—viewers can start, stop, reverse or advance slide show

- Available exclusively to **eBay Picture Services users**

- Fee: 75 cents per listing

You can see that the slide show method of placing pictures on your title adds focus, detail and professionalism that you can't beat for getting buyers interested.

Our discounted package offers you maximum exposure:

- Add up to six pictures
- Supersize all your pictures (up to 800w x 600h pixels (11" x 8"))!
- Display your listing in the eBay <u>Gallery</u>
- Available exclusively to eBay Picture Services users
- Fee: $1.00 (a $1.75 value)

Creativity Counts!

It is important to write an ad that paints a picture with words. Have you heard the saying, "A picture is worth a thousand words?" It is true. Write your ad that paints a beautiful picture of your item that buyers cannot resist. If you are selling homemade doll clothes for Barbie, play it up. Write in your ad how these hand crafted Barbie outfits are one of a kind and cannot be found anywhere else. Anyone who is looking for special Barbie clothes will surely take a peek at what you have to offer IF you describe it in those terms.

"**HANDCRAFTED BARBIE** Clothes and Accessories **ONE OF A KIND!**"

If you are selling teddy bears, put something in the ad that this special teddy bear is looking for a good home, and a kind person to love and take care of him. People will be more likely to place a bid on your item if you convey a bit of your personality. Be upbeat, creative and this will endear you to your buyers.

NEWSLETTER ADVERTISING

Creating your own newsletter on your website is another way of advertising your business. It can be time consuming, but well worth the effort.

I think it is understood that a newsletter is a powerful marketing tool. Any promotions you send to your customers and subscribers after they've been receiving your newsletters will be that much more successful because with your newsletter, you'll have:

- Established your credibility,
- Developed a reputation as an industry expert,
- Cultivated a relationship with your subscribers,
- Inspired customer loyalty,
- And maintained regular contact.

Regularly give your subscribers useful or entertaining information that they'll benefit from, and they'll come to trust you, respect you and buy from you.

Sounds great, right? But now you're probably left wondering, "How do I get people to subscribe?" After all, you can write hundreds of newsletters, but if you only have a handful of subscribers, it can be a lot of work for little reward.

The big mistake I see a lot of e-business owners making is thinking that simply posting a "Subscribe today" box on their Web sites—and then forgetting about it—is going to attract subscribers by the thousands. Even if your Web site is highly trafficked, this is going to produce disappointing results. You need to be prepared to actively promote your newsletter, much the same way you would promote any other product or service online. Try following these steps to increase your subscriber base:

> **Step 1:** Promote your newsletter on your Web site. Yes, you should definitely promote your newsletter on your site. But the keyword here is "promote." How motivating is it for a visitor to give you his or her name and e-mail address when presented with a subscribe box titled, "Subscribe to our free newsletter"?

> Why should they subscribe? How will they benefit from subscribing? What are they going to get? Just because your newsletter is "free" doesn't mean they'll want it. There are plenty of free newsletters out there they could subscribe to. What makes yours different or special?

You really need to "sell" your free newsletter to potential subscribers. In one or two short, exciting sentences clearly state the benefits of subscribing to your newsletter. For example, if your Web site is golf related, you might say something like "Subscribe to the FREE 'Golf Tips' newsletter and receive monthly tips and advice from Pro Golfers. Improve your swing, hear about world-renowned golf courses, learn which clubs the experts prefer, plus much more!" It sounds a lot more interesting than "Subscribe to my free newsletter," don't you think? Visitors to your web site will think so, too!

The other tip I'd like to share is about where you should place your newsletter subscription box on your site. First of all, don't hide it! Your goal should be to make sure that everyone who visits your site is offered the opportunity to subscribe to your newsletter at least once, if not twice.

Your newsletter subscription box should appear "above the fold" (i.e., it should be immediately visible on the first screen) of your homepage. This is where you'll get the best response—and the most subscribers!

Step 2: Offer existing customers a subscription. Have you offered your existing customers a subscription to your newsletter? If you haven't, you should e-mail them an offer like this as soon as possible. This is an easy way to get a flood of new subscriptions.
And be sure to add a subscription offer to your "thank you for ordering" page or e-mail. If someone's interested enough in your product or service to purchase it, you can bet they'll want to subscribe to your newsletter. Don't miss this opportunity to maintain contact with existing customers.

And be sure to add a subscription offer to your "thank you for ordering" page or e-mail. If someone's interested enough in your product or service to purchase it, you can bet they'll want to subscribe to your newsletter. Don't miss this opportunity to maintain contact with existing customers.

If you've offered a free subscription to your customers but received a poor response, consider making things a little more interesting by offering them a "special gift" like a free article or ebook when they subscribe. This extra incentive should dramatically boost the number of new subscriptions you receive.

Step 3: Promote your newsletter in your e-mail signatures. An electronic signature—also referred to as a "sig file"—is a three-to six-line footer you can attach to the bottom of your e-mail messages and public forum postings. And it's a prime spot to advertise your newsletter.

Unlike a lot of other blatant advertisements, a sig file is universally accepted, so take advantage of this perfect opportunity to plug your newsletter. Anyone who receives e-mail from you will also receive your invitation to subscribe to your newsletter. Chances are that if you're e-mailing them, they already have a direct interest in your industry or niche, so take advantage of this and offer them a free subscription right at the bottom of any e-mail you send.

Step 4: Ad swap with other newsletters and e-zines. A great trick for increasing your subscriber base involves contacting other newsletters that relate to your target market and offering to swap ads with them. Tell the newsletter owners you'll promote their newsletter to your subscriber base if they'll return the favor. This is a great way for both of you to increase your readership. Subscribers will appreciate the recommendation of another source of quality information, and as long as the sites you swap with are complementary and not competitive, it's not going to hurt your business at all.

Step 5: Promote your newsletter in newsgroups, discussion lists and forum postings. Another good place to promote your newsletter and locate targeted potential subscribers is in newsgroups, discussion lists and forums that relate directly to your industry or niche. Simply post a brief description of your newsletter and a link to your subscription page.

Step 6: Offer subscribers the opportunity to give gift subscriptions. Offer or announce gift subscriptions in your newsletter that encourage your current subscribers to send gift subscriptions to friends. You can automate your site to send the gift subscription with a little blurb stating whom the gift is from and what they'll be receiving (and the opportunity to unsubscribe, of course). A friend of mine has built most of his mailing list doing this alone. He went from 5,000 subscribers to more than 16,000 subscribers in less than a year just using this one technique.

Step 7: Renting opt-in e-mail lists. Renting e-mail addresses from third-party list providers is a route that some new newsletter owners choose because you're given quick access to a list of hundreds, if not thousands, of people who have "opted" to receive e-mail on topics that interest them. You can usually expect to be charged 5 to 20 cents per deliverable message, and you should expect any e-mail addresses that are "bad" or that "bounce" to be replaced by addresses that are current.

If you decide to use a service like this, it's absolutely critical that you find out how the e-mail addresses were obtained. You want e-mail addresses that have been collected ethically and responsibly, and this means you want the e-mail addresses of people who are directly interested in your product, industry or field of expertise, and have given their permission and "opted-in" to the list.

Important note: If you buy lists of e-mail addresses that have been "harvested" from newsgroups, classified ad sites, online services and other similar sources, you'll be accused of spamming! These people have not given you permission to contact them, and you can get into a lot of trouble this way. Again, I can't overstate the importance of making sure the e-mail addresses you rent have been collected ethically and responsibly!

A few reputable third-party list providers who offer targeted opt-in e-mail lists are:

Postmaster Direct, YesMail, E-Target, Targ-it, Focalex and TargitMail.

Ultimately, your goal should be to develop a relationship with your subscribers through quality articles in your newsletter before you even consider trying to sell them anything. Give them quality information that they'll benefit from to establish your credibility and develop a rapport with them.

Remember that the true value lies in the relationship that you develop with the person who owns the e-mail address—not in the e-mail address itself. It will be the relationship you develop with your subscribers that will result in big sales both now and in the future—an important point to keep in mind no matter how many new subscribers you attract.

Successful Sellers

Here are some success stories from actual eBay sellers. Their real names are not used on the eBay site to protect confidentiality. By entering their user numbers, you can access their ID cards, which will give you a report card of their selling practices, what they sell, and what ratings they have gotten from satisfied or dissatisfied buyers. Every seller gets a report card made up of comments received from buyers. If you are an honest, conscientious seller, your report card will be a great asset in driving buyers to your store or auction. Obviously, the better rating you have, the greater amount of people will trust you.

"Lopebaby"

How long have you been using eBay and what do you use it for?
I have been using eBay for a little over three years now. I mostly sell books, clothes and toys, but I also use it to buy stuff in order to get great deals. I love saving money, and eBay is the number one place to do that!

How often do you visit or surf the site?

I get on eBay at least three times a day. More if I have items up for sale. I am addicted to checking my bids.

- **If you mainly use eBay to sell items, do you have a certain strategy that helps you to sell the items that you really want to sell?** Well, my strategy is always to list everything as honestly as possible, and to start all my items out as low as I can possibly go to give buyers the best deal they can get. I also try to take great pictures and give plenty of information without dragging on too much. Don't charge too much for shipping, and accept personal checks!!!

- **What tips would you give to people out there who are selling their items?**
  Honesty is the number one priority, Great pictures is number two

- **Tell us how your Feedback rating has improved your reputation?**
  I think it really helps that I have a high feedback rating with no negatives. I know I like the sellers I buy from to have a reputable feedback rating.

- **Can you give us a brief description of what eBay means to you?**
  eBay means I can stay home with my kids and still help with the finances also. It also has shown me that there are a lot of kind, caring and understanding people out there from all over the world.

WanderWonder # 1283

- **How long have you been using eBay and what do you use it for?**
  I have been a seller on eBay for over 3 years now. At this time, it is my sole occupation. I use eBay for both buying & selling, and for meeting great people around the world! I use eBay mainly as a seller, specifically of gems & minerals.

- **What is the most unique thing that you have sold?**
  My eBay career started when I found an old rock collection at a roadside sale. None of the minerals were identified or labeled, so I listed them on eBay as Mystery Rocks. They sold like hotcakes! I was so amazed with the success of my "Mystery Rocks" that I began listing other items. I still sell Mystery Rocks (not the same ones, of course!) and my customers seem to think they're as much fun as I do!

- **Do you have a certain strategy that helps you to sell the items that you really want to sell?**
  I don't think I have a selling "strategy," exactly. I am ultra-honest in my ads, with an attitude that leans toward understatement. I would rather under-sell than over-hype! I try to pick the best overall category for my items—I tend to stay out of sub-sub-categories where they might be overlooked. My best selling strategy, though, is customer service. I value my customers, not just as buyers, but also as potential friends. Many of them now are!

- **What tips would you give to people out there who are selling their items?**
  For new members of the eBay community, I would counsel patience, honesty, and courtesy. It may be tempting to "blow your stack" when a transaction isn't going your way, but a cool head & a polite tone can really make a difference. For me, communication is everything. I recommend keeping your transaction "partner" informed of every step taken, whether buying or selling.

- **Tell us how your Feedback rating has improved your reputation?**
  Feedback is an absolute joy to me. Some days when I'm feeling low, I check my profile just to read all the nice things people have said! I consider feedback to be the single most important feature of eBay. My reputation is built on excellent service & quality goods, and my customers can see that in my feedback. I am very proud that I have so

few negs, and I work hard to solve any problems before they become complaints.

- **How has eBay changed your life?**
  Where do I begin? Before I found eBay, I was a complete technophobe! I couldn't turn on a computer, and had no idea what www.com meant. Then my Dad found eBay, and started making a living from home. Well, if my Dad could do it, so could I! I got a laptop, found some "Mystery Rocks", and within 3 months learned to write HTML & quit my minimum wage job. *Now I have more time for my family, less stress, and a pretty decent income. Yay, eBay!*

Mr. and Mrs. Mike Waters

My wife & I have been selling on Ebay for about 5 years. I have collected antiques all my adult life and occasionally had the need to sell off the excess, I had heard rumors about a new internet site that put sellers in touch with collectors all over the country and made it easy to sell. I tried Ebay and soon realized it would change everything. We sold a few things at first and had terrific results. 3 years ago I retired from my career in construction and began to make the transition to work full time in the antiques business largely selling on Ebay. We are approaching our 2nd anniversary doing this business full time and we are having a ball doing it. Advice...it is a job, be prepared to work hard if you want to succeed, find your niche and be good at it, give your customers a high level of service because without them you are nothing. Because they know how important it is to be honest, courteous and forthright, their feedback report cards are the best. This is what your feedback record should look like.

eb Y ID card	interestingproducts (1265) ⭐
Member since: Thursday, Sep 14, 2000 Location: Canada	

Summary of Most Recent Comments

	Past 7 days	Past month	Past 6 mo.
Positive	13	50	343
Neutral	0	0	1
Negative	0	0	0
Total	13	50	344
Bid Retractions	0	0	0

You can see from just these three testimonials that is it a fact that people can actually quit their day jobs in time and become very successful. These people are also having fun and finding greater rewards doing what they want and love to do.

Setting Up

After you have registered for your sellers account, you will be asked to set up a valid eBay payment account with your credit/debit card and checking account. If you don't want to give this information, use the "become ID verified" option. Register for eBay Payments or Pay Pal, which enables you to take credit cards from buyers. Most buying is done with credit cards. Using eBay, you don't have to apply and qualify for a merchant account. Pay Pal takes a small fee for every transaction, but it is worth it. The fees depend on the price you are selling an item. You must tack on Pay Pal's or eBay Payments percentage onto your retail price or your profits will go down.

For example: you are selling a custom made teddy bear for $135.00. Pay Pal's fee for the transaction is 1.5%. They will take from your $135.00 selling price that $2.03 cents. You must find out what the exact percentage is that they will deduct from your selling price. You will add $2.03 to the $135.00 you are charging your buyer. This way, you recoup the fee. $2.03 may not seem like much, but it adds up as you begin to sell many items.

Paying Your eBay Seller Fees

There are three ways to pay eBay fees:

- **eBay Direct Pay:** The easiest and most convenient way to make payment on your eBay account. Simply provide eBay with your checking account number and bank routing number, and eBay will automatically deduct your monthly invoice amount from your account. Once you sign for eBay Direct Pay, your bank account will be debited on a fixed day of the month dependent on your billing cycle. To sign up for eBay Direct Pay or update your checking account information, just complete the safe and easy form. **This option is only available to users billed in U.S. dollars with bank accounts in the United States.**

- You may also make a one-time eBay Direct Pay payment.
- **Credit Card on File:** You can place your credit card (Visa, MasterCard, American Express or Discover Card) on your eBay account for regular monthly payments. Each month eBay will automatically charge your invoice amount directly to your credit card on file. Your credit card will normally be charged 7 to 10 days after receipt of your invoice. <u>Place your credit card on file</u> for automatic

monthly billing or update your current credit card information. You may also make a <u>one-time credit card payment.</u>

> •   Check and Money Order Payment: When making payment by check
>
>   and/or money order you must submit a payment coupon along with your
>
>   check/money order and mail it to the address on the form.
>
> You may request and print a payment coupon.
>
> eBay requires payment in full each month on accounts with a balance of $1.00 or greater.

A billing cycle is assigned to your seller account when you create the account. This billing cycle determines your payment-due date (called your Billing Cycle Date). Your Billing Cycle Date is clearly displayed at the top of your <u>Account Status</u> page. This date will also appear on your invoice as your Invoice Date. Please check your account status to verify your Billing Cycle Date.

You will usually be invoiced within five days of your Billing Cycle Date via email. This invoice will include your previous month's account activity as well as any past due amounts. Please check your <u>Account Status</u> for your current account balance.

Failure to Make Payment on Your eBay Account

eBay requires payment in full each month on accounts with balances of $1.00 or greater. You will be billed a monthly finance charge of 1.5% or the highest amount permitted by applicable law—whichever is lower—if your account becomes past due. Your account may be suspended for non-payment, and you may be responsible for collection costs.

Shipping and Handling Costs

On your storefront or auction information, you will have to show if you pay for shipping and handling or do you expect the buyer to pay it? Of course, unless you want to go in the hole each time you sell something, the buyer needs to incur that expense. What you should charge for this depends on what you are selling. If you sell big heavy things like original, framed paintings, your shipping and handling would be significantly more than if you were selling buttons. I suggest you invest in a postal scale so you will know how much your item(s) weigh. You can get a price per ounce/pound table from the Post Office. You will then be able to give an accurate estimate for postage.

Handling is another matter. If you are selling fragile items you will have to invest in appropriate packaging materials. Your item must arrive to its destination intact and without damage. Sellers who don't give as much care to their shipping and handling issues will pay eventually. Buyers will give you a much less than perfect on your sellers report card. Everyone expects their bought items to arrive in perfect condition. It is no less on eBay. When listing your prices, you can either incorporate your shipping and handling charges, or list them separately. If you are adding in shipping to your sales price, you must add the cost of shipping to it. Never eat the shipping and handling chargers. You will go broke.

Packaging materials can prove costly. Here are a few tips for finding free shipping materials from Lace and Leather Online!

The United States Post Office is still "pushing" their Priority Mail services.

You can order all the shipping supplies you want through the USPS— order in minutes on line—and have them delivered to your door. When you make your first order, the USPS will mail you a postcard to sign and mail back to them. The "payment" for this deal is simply agreeing to (and signing to prove it) use these supplies only for their intended purpose. Anyone caught turning Priority Mail boxes inside out to use a cheaper mail service will be in big trouble. We haven't done this so we don't know if you get a large fine, jail time, or just lose the privilege to ever receive any more supplies. So, this is not for you if you prefer to send your packages by UPS or using the Book Rate.

Just what kind of supplies does the USPS offer? Small boxes, larger boxes, flat boxes, larger flat boxes, small flat boxes, flat mailers, "Priority Mail" tape, and labels. You can't have it all; you have to buy your own bubble wrap! The only real catch is that you must order the minimum, which can be a case of boxes. Since the boxes come flat, this is not as bad as it sounds.

For those that don't want to use Priority Mail or the USPS in general, there are still places to get boxes free.

- Your local supermarket gets deliveries at least once a week. Just ask one of their employees on what day and at what time their deliveries arrive. They won't usually save boxes for you, but you can walk in and get as many as you like before they cut them down for recycling.

- Office Depot has great boxes for larger items. They receive their reams of paper in sturdy boxes with lids, and these are always clean. Our local Office Depot receives paper deliveries twice a week. The store manager even agreed to hold the boxes for a few hours. We just need to go in on the correct day. Since these are such handy boxes, you may have to be the first to get to the store to beat others with the same idea.

- Check the free ads in the Recycler. Companies go out of business all the time, and they would usually prefer to give their supply of boxes away than to pay someone to haul them away. We found a vitamin store that was closing down and got hundreds of small and tiny boxes. These are not only great for mailing small items, but they are perfect for double boxing a set of smaller breakables.

- Liquor stores have the sturdiest boxes since bottles of liquor and wine are so heavy. If you sell bottles, these may even come with cardboard slots in them already to keep bottles from hitting each other when you send out several to one buyer.

eBay Insertion Fees

For being able to use eBay's many custom tools which enable a seller to have a professional storefront, eBay charges insertion fees. Here is a chart for fees by number of items.

- Store Inventory Listings are fixed price listings that only appear within your eBay Store, and will not appear in eBay Search or Listings. But, buyers can search and browse within your Store to find these items

- The insertion fee covers any quantity for a single listing, whether you list 1 or 1,000 of the same item. The fees vary based on the duration of your listing.

Auction Listings Fees

	Insertion Fee	Surcharge	Total
3, 5, 7, 10, 20 days	$0.05	N/A	$0.05
30 days	$0.05	N/A	$0.05
60 days	$0.05	$0.05	$0.10
90 days	$0.05	$0.10	$0.15
120 days	$0.05	$0.15	$0.20
Good 'Till Cancelled	$0.05/ 30 days	N/A	$0.05/ 30 days

- Auction listings appear in your Auction listings appear in your eBay Store as well as in eBay Search and Listings pages.

- There are no additional insertion fees to have your eBay auctions included in your store; when you pay the standard eBay insertion fee to list an auction, the item will automatically appear in your eBay Store. Auctions that were listed before your store was opened will not appear in your store. Please see the eBay Fees page for more detailed information.

- A $0.05 feature fee will be charged for all auction items listed with the Buy it Now feature. Please see the eBay Fees page for more detailed information.

Final Value Items

On the final sale price (final value) of your item, the Fee structure is the same for both fixed price and auction listings.

Closing Value	Final Value Fee
$0 - $25	5.25% of the closing value
$25 - $1,000	5.25% of the initial $25 ($1.31), plus 2.75% of the remaining closing value balance.
Over $1,000	5.25% of the initial $25 ($1.31), plus 2.75% of the initial $25-$1000 ($26.81), plus 1.50% of the remaining closing value balance.

If your item sold for $25 or less, your Final Value Fee is 5.25% of the final sale price. For items that sell for over $25.00, see the fee schedule at http://pages.ebay.com/storefronts/pricing.html.

Also visit http://pages.ebay.com/help/sellerguide/selling-fees.html#BIN. The fees may seem high, but they are actually in tune when you consider all of the structures and tools eBay provides.

Protect Yourself

Rarely does anything go wrong with your venture on eBay. But it is always wise to protect your investment—your business. Here are some tips on keeping your business going strong by being safe with who you sell to and keeping your experience as positive as it can be.

- Represent the items you are selling fairly and accurately.
- Respond promptly to buyer questions.
- Review your buyer's feedback.
- Clearly state your return policy on your listing.

- Ship with a **tracking number and insurance**. This procedure can help resolve disputes in cases where a buyer claims to have never received an item or received a broken item.

- Maintain records of shipping receipts as proof the item was shipped.

- Only ship items to the **verified billing address** on the buyer's credit card account (if applicable).

- **Verify payment** before shipping items (including holding checks until they clear).

- Keep copies of any proof of your item's authenticity.

- Use extra caution with:

   International Shipping

   Revised Shipping Information requested by buyer

   Unknown or new buyers

   Unusual bidding activity

   Orders shipped rush or overnight

- Try to establish contact with the buyer immediately after auction or store sale ends.

- Establish a timeframe with buyer, making it clear how long you will wait for payment, and what type of payment you will accept.

- Make sure to state your rules in the auction regarding what types of bidders you will accept (For example, "no bidders with negative feedback," or "new bidders with 0 feedback must contact the seller.")

Most buyers are serious and conduct their business in an upright, honest manner. However, there are always the other types. Since everyone must register to buy or sell, eBay requires all buyers to sign in and keep a record of the transactions they make. Sellers can also report any wrongdoing or shady practices of any buyers. Therefore, you are able to check out anyone who wishes to buy from you. Just as in a "real" store, you have the right to not accept business from anyone.

What if I can't reach my buyer?

Like you, buyers sometimes have emergencies, illnesses, or computer problems. Check your buyer's feedback to see what other trading partners have said. If your buyer has mostly positive feedback with little or no mention of problems, be patient. Your buyer may not be able to respond to you right away for legitimate reasons.

If you don't get an email response, you can request your buyer's phone number. Sometimes a phone call helps make communication easier.

If your item was a regular listing that ended without a reserve price or a Reserve Price Auction where the reserve is met and you are unable to contact your winning buyer, your listing may fall under eBay's Non-paying Buyer Policy. This policy will tell you how to request a fee credit from eBay if your buyer does not pay.

You can see that eBay takes special care to protect you, the seller. You also have access to a special site with live help should you encounter a problem with a buyer that you cannot solve. This is also true with every other conflict you may have in your selling experience. Remember too that your credit card issuer, shipping insurance and eBay's Fraud Protection Program can help you recover funds lost in a transaction.

Choose Your Selling Format

Choose which selling format you want. The classic auction-bidding format is the most popular. You collect bids from buyers for a fixed amount of days, up to ten days. Buy It Now is an icon on your listing where buyers can buy for that amount and no more bidding takes place. Fixed price option sets a certain price and no bidding takes place. Buyers purchase your item immediately.

It is important to write good titles and choose which category is best for what you are selling. The more concise your titles, the easier it will be for your buyers to find you. Note the area from which you are selling. People would surprise you in your local vicinity that might be looking for the items you are offering.

Sometimes it's obvious what buyers are going to want to know about an item. If it's a concert, they want to know which city it's in and who is playing. If it's a computer, they want to know what brand it is and how much RAM it has. Item specifics make it easy for sellers and buyers to use this standardized information to connect.

Filling in all the Item Specifics fields is to your advantage, because it:

- Gives buyers an easy, fast way to search for your item
- Makes the basic facts about your item clear and accessible on your listing

When you fill in the Item Specifics fields, buyers browsing your item's category will get a handy menu like the one below to help them search for items by their attributes. This precise search method brings appropriate buyers to your listing, fast! eBay has a search window like the one below in which buyers can easily find what they are looking for. It's important that you give very specific titles for your items so that you can easily be found.

Use of the Item Specifics is optional, however it is definitely to your benefit to complete as many of the details as are applicable. Buyers using

Item Specifics to search for an item may not find your item if the Item Specifics are left blank

Please be mindful of the information you provide via Item Specifics. This information will be displayed above your item description and is considered a **binding** part of your item description to buyers.

Do you need to include the item specifics information in your item description as well?

By browsing to a specific category or by searching on items that are located mostly in a certain category, buyers will be presented with a Product Finder on the search-results and browse pages. The Product Finder is unique for each category that uses item specifics. The buyer selects the item specifics values of interest and then performs a search using these values

For example, the Item Specifics available in the Tickets category may be related to Date and Location of event, while the Item Specifics in the Laptops category could refer to Brand and Speed of computer. For teddy bears, your item specifics could refer to custom, handmade, vintage, holiday bears, etc.

Your buyers can go to the help center to type in the product or service they are looking for. The descriptions that are most near to the product is what will appear in the search results. So if you are selling antique broach jewelry, don't specify "jewelry" in your item specifics. You want your buyer to get to be able to find your product with ease, not having to search thousands of listings of which they may never get to your item. Instead, describe your jewelry just as it is—antique broaches.

Listings using Item Specifics are more likely to sell, and at prices 10% higher than others, on average. This performance represents an average based on recent transactions. No representation is made that the final price or conversion rate of a specific item will increase by the average percentages noted here.

You can see how important it is to take your time deciding how you will accurately describe your items. The idea is to help buyers easily find you.

EBay also enables you to set up a store in which you can place multiple merchandise for different prices. Sales are accomplished right away so there is no waiting. Your eBay store must be set up in that format instead of as an auction. But you can have links from your auctions to your store, and vice versa. Additional advertising must be placed elsewhere in order for your customers to find you.

When a buyer finds your item listing, there is also a link, "view seller's other items" to better insure that your multiple listings aren't lost in the cracks.

Every listing page has two links to let buyers send a question to the seller. One is the seller's User ID itself. The other is at the end of the next line below the seller info. By clicking on either link, the buyer will get a form that will send an email to the seller.

Buyers must be registered and approved by eBay in order to send you e-mail. This is a built in protection service for the seller so that you get only serious questions and comments from dedicated buyers.

Here is some good advice from one of eBay's best information assistants, Jim Griffith:

"However, there is an important consideration eBay Store sellers must note about eBay Store items—they do not show up in a regular Title Search. There is a special Title Search for eBay Store items, but since most eBay buyers use the regular Title Search to find items on eBay, a seller who places all their items in an eBay Store may find that traffic to their items decreases.

"Instead of listing all your items in your eBay Store, reserve a selection of items and put them up for sale in a regular, non-eBay Store listing, either in the fixed price or auction-style format. Make sure that within all your item descriptions you have a prominent link to your eBay Store. That way, you can use a regular eBay listing to drive traffic to your eBay Store items.

"Also, if you are using an eBay Store, you should take advantage of Merchandising Manager. This excellent eBay feature is free for all eBay Store sellers. It allows you to establish connections between your regular eBay listings and your eBay Store items so that you can "cross promote" all your eBay items, regardless of listing format. "

With Merchandising Manager, you select the items you want to feature and the relationships you want to create between them. Then, each time a buyer bids on or buys one of your items, up to three of your other related items are promoted in two places: on the Bid Confirmation page and during Checkout In addition, if you are a featured or anchor Store seller your merchandise selections will also appear on each of your listing pages.

Welcome to eBay Workshops...

Workshops are board events presented by Community Development, special guests—even expert eBay members—on a myriad of eBay-related subjects. Workshops combine "lecture" material with interactive discussion. They are a great way to learn, interact with eBay staff, and chat with the experts on a wide variety of interesting subjects. eBay's workshops are just like the training you would get if you were to buy a franchise! A list of upcoming workshops can be found at:
http://members.ebay.com/aboutme/workshopevents/?ssPageName=C MDV:IC1350

Listing Policies for Sellers
Know The Rules!

Familiarize yourself with eBay's listing policies before posting an item. You'll have a safe and fun selling experience knowing that your listing complies with community standards and guidelines.

Listings that violate eBay's policies may result in disciplinary action. This action may include a formal warning, the ending of all violating listings, or even temporary or indefinite suspension of a user's account. eBay will consider the circumstances of an alleged offense and the user's trading records before taking action. In most cases, eBay will credit all associated fees when a listing is ended.

Sales Outside of eBay

- Using member contact information obtained from eBay or using any eBay feature to offer to sell an item outside of eBay to any of your bidders in a Reserve Not Met listing.

- Listings of catalogs from which buyers may directly order items are prohibited. In these situations, the seller will typically offer the catalog for low bid prices and complete sales outside of eBay for items found in the catalog.

The eBay item page cannot refer to or promote the seller's individual Web site, or other businesses. Sellers cannot use eBay members or their listings to create mailing lists for other business use.

It's important to know the rules so that you can build a business for yourself that will become reliable and consistent. A good reputation is vital.

Your eBay Storefront

Why open your own eBay Storefront? The advantages are enormous!

✓ **Attract New Customers**—eBay has over 42 million registered users

✓ **Sell More**—Existing eBay sellers see an increase in overall sales when they open an eBay Store

✓ **Get Extra Promotion**—eBay automatically promotes Your Store and items on and off eBay through eBay's partnerships with the top search engines

✓ **Customize your Look & Feel**—Personalize Your Store! Add custom colors, photos and give potential buyers detailed information about your items.

✓ **Feature your Brand, Products & Expertise**—Create up to 11 custom categories to market and merchandise—with the Merchandising Manager you have the ability to control cross-selling at the item level.

✓ **Get a Search Engine Devoted to Your Products**

Your Store comes with it's own search engine, so buyers can search just within your inventory

✓ **Build a Place on eBay Where Buyers can Return to Shop**—You receive a custom URL for your eBay Store and buyers can easily bookmark your Store as a favorite.

✓ **It's Fast & Easy**—In less than 15 minutes, you can set up your Store through a simple, on-line form

✓ **It's Affordable**

You can choose from three subscription plans based on your business needs, starting at $9.95 per month. Plus, **your first 30 days are free.**

You have several different options when setting up an eBay Storefront. You are given a 30-day free trial for any option you choose so that you can make an informed decision as to which format is best for your needs.

It can become difficult to keep up with all of your e-mails from customers with questions about your products or general comments. Hopefully, your mailbox will be constantly full because that means you are making money! <u>Sellers Assistant Basic</u> helps you with professional listings, tracking, and email management for a small fee of $4.99 per month. For $15.99, you can get the <u>Pro</u>, which helps with total business management, bulk listings and post-sale assignments. With both of these business tools, you get e-mail management, sales tracking at a glance, ability to post pictures of your products, and help with formatting and HTML. eBay will give you a 30 day free trial of either the <u>Basic</u> or <u>Pro</u> versions of the <u>Sellers Assistant</u> so you can try both to see which one suits you best.

There are other store features in which eBay will manage your items, inventory, listings, advertising and e-mail management at levels all the way up to $499.99 a month. Obviously, you will start with the basic until your sales can afford to hire eBay to further promote and manage your store. Many sellers have reached the kinds of sales that warrant three figures management. *When* you get to that point, you will want these services or you won't have any time to enjoy all of that extra income! The cool thing about having your own store is that it looks like a professional marketplace that people can have confidence in buying from you.

Merchandising Your Store

You have researched and chosen the best products or services that you can provide and which buyers will want to buy.

Your Store lets you use your Custom Categories (up to 11) to help build "aisles" within your store for buyers to shop. Some storefront owners have used product-based categories (e.g., ceramics, glassware, posters) while others use more flexible categories (e.g., sale items, seasonal, best-sellers, etc.) People are usually looking for a certain item and don't want to search through product-based categories to find exactly what they are looking for. You can also promote new items in a special category (e.g., Specials of the week, hot items, etc.) Having well done photos of your items, products or services is a must. People want to see what they are buying. The better your descriptions and photos, the more buyers you will have.

Build your brand and reputation

- Buyers will have more confidence if you have a clear and professional store policy on your page. It should clearly describe how you run your store in regards to orders, refunds (if any), your contact information, pricing, and problem solving, etc.

- Use a custom logo and build a professional-looking About My Store page that tells buyers about your business and your business practices. Need help designing a logo? eBay will help you craft one that is just right.

- On your store, list all of the items that are also listed in your auctions. This is called *cross selling*. You should have good descriptions and include accessories, and have a greater breadth of selection. For example, if you make baskets, also offer liners and personalization. This will increase sales and interest.

- Be sure to mention your store in all of your eBay Listings

- Use the Merchandising Manager to cross-sell your items at the item level, and promote these items in key buyer locations. Your advertising options are vast. Use them.

A Store seller who has listed a camera, for example, may wish to show buyers the film, camera case and batteries that goes along with it. <u>Featured</u>

and <u>Anchor Store</u> sellers will have the added benefit of having this merchandise also show up on their View Item pages too! That page will look like this with all of the pertinent information regarding your item(s).

http://cgi.ebay.com/ws/eBayISAPI.dll?ViewItem&category=802&item=752616846

You will have several options for using the <u>Merchandising Manager</u>. If you don't sell items that have accessories, such as baskets with inserts or watches with optional faces, for example, you won't need the Merchandising Manager.

Promote your store in your Auctions

- Create a balanced inventory of auction and store items on eBay— The most successful store sellers are using auction items to help drive traffic to their store

- Mention your eBay Store in your auction listing descriptions (e.g., "We have more great inventory & accessories you can BUY NOW from our eBay Store")

- Suggest that buyers visit your store for accessories, add-ons, or more colors and sizes of your items

- Use the <u>Merchandising Manager</u> to cross-sell your items at the item level, and promote these items in key buyer locations

- Offer promotions such as free or discounted shipping on additional items they purchase from your store in the same day

Build brand awareness with buyers

- To insure repeat buyers, which is of utmost importance, always include a business card with all your shipments and communications with your buyers and potential buyers. For example, "We at (store name) appreciate your business. Please visit us often for weekly and new products at (your store URL). Include a link to custom categories.

- Include your store URL and logo on your business cards and packing slips

- Advertising is the number one priority. If it looks professional, you will be perceived of the same caliber of retailer of any department store or business in the "real" world.

Word of mouth

- Encourage your family, friends, associates, and off-eBay customers to visit your eBay Store, and ask them to spread the word to their friends. Word of mouth advertising is one of the best methods to get traffic to your store. By the same token, if you are dishonest and do not pay attention to your buyers input, your shady business practices will also follow you by word of mouth.

You have an amazing opportunity to advertise your business on eBay. Advertical is auctioning off millions of ad impressions on the eBay.com website. Imagine the recognition you'll get with your name in lights on one of the world's most popular websites. eBay will list your ad at the top of your category-listing page, giving you premium ad space.

The Instrument Guy

— *"[Stores] provide the little guy with a low cost venue for marketing world wide as well as gaining selling power and exposure."*

| www.stores.ebay.com/theinstrumentguy | —Michael Pagliaro |

GemProf

— *"I love the pictorial review combination of auctions and store items. This way the customer can see everything that you have in one location."*

| www.ebaystores.com/gemprof | —Eva M. Ananiewicz |

Scripophily

— *"The eBay Store is a great way to sell products 24 hours a day and you can come to work when you please."*

| www.ebaystores.com/scripophilycom | —Bob Kerstien |

A seller may not allow buyers to choose from a selection of items. This practice can lead to misrepresentation or fraud because it requires offline negotiation

Giveaways, raffles, or prizes

Listings that promote giveaways, random drawings, or prizes are not permitted. Such promotions are highly regulated and may be unlawful in many states.

Listings may not circumvent eBay's fees. Examples include:

- Offering the **opportunity to buy** the listed item or other item outside of eBay
- Low prices but **unreasonably high shipping** or **handling costs**
- Listing an item that **requires or offers additional purchase**

Multiple Items Listing avoidance: listing a single item and offering additional identical items for sale in the item description. In these situations, the seller typically instructs buyers to indicate the number of items they want, and states that they can get the same price as the item in the listing.

eBay itself may run such promotions and may grant authorization to its partners or third-party companies to run such promotions.

As you can see, there are rules that must be adhered to in order to have the best selling experience and make the most money. EBay's rules are for your safety as well as for the buyers.

Monthly Sales Reports

Now Anchor and Featured Store sellers receive monthly reports on their sales. Stores Seller Reporting provides sellers with both seller-specific and marketplace performance data. Best of all, Stores Seller Reporting is free to Anchor and Featured Stores. All Anchor and Featured Store Sellers will be emailed the reports to the email address associated with their Store Account. This feature makes it easier for you to keep track of your business without having to take a class in bookkeeping or accounting.

DROP SHIPPING—Another concept to consider

We have talked about selecting an item you like to make yourself as well as items you may have stored away that you no longer want. Now, I want to talk about another opportunity for selling. Many people have gotten into the wholesale or drop shipping method, and it has proven to be very successful.

There is more than one way to make a super successful eBay enterprise. This is called drop shipping. The whole point of starting an e-commerce business is to make money. That's something you must not lose sight of.

There's a great opportunity for people to find products to sell without investing a single penny in inventory—by drop shipping. It's the perfect way to start in Internet business on a shoestring budget.

Drop-shipping is a product delivery mechanism that allows you to sell merchandise without inventory. The great benefit of drop-shipping is that it eliminates packing expenses. You make the sale and collect retail price and then send orders to a drop-shipper, and pay much lower wholesale prices, they fulfill your orders by shipping merchandise directly to your customers. You will have no risks of stocking inventory.

And the wholesaler will drop ship the product for you! All you have to do is collect the payment (in your Merchant or Pay pal account—full instructions are given to have this up and running in just 10 minutes), pay the wholesaler, and tell him where to ship the product. Oh, and keep the profit for yourself, of course.

Here are just a few examples of the kind of products you can buy and the prices you can buy them for:

Cell Phone Boosters	$.17
80GB Hard Drive	$83.54
Butane Lighters	$.99
Extreme Power Plus	$4.25
Chronograph Watch	$2.99
Hands Free Cell Phone	$2.69
Gucci Watches	$22.99
Viacreme	$8.91
4 pack of AA batteries	$.66
Leather Jackets	$18.66
Stacker 3	$5.15
Leather Purse	$6.38

So you have the perfect business. Just consider this:

Start-up capital—	NIL
Premises—	None required
Employees—	NIL
Stock/Inventory—	NIL
Running costs—	Practically nil—just the listing fees on eBay or whatever online auction you use (some auctions are actually free to list on)
Risk—	Non-existent
Other overheads—	NIL

If you've been interested in starting your own Internet business, but you've been trying to avoid the hassles of things like developing and producing products, tracking your inventory, setting up warehouse space, and maintaining a confusing shipping/receiving infrastructure, then drop shipping may be the answer.

Drop shipping is simply an arrangement between you and the manufacturer or distributor of a product you wish to sell in which the manufacturer or distributor—not you—ships the product to your customers. This means you can sell quality, brand-name products on your Web site for a hefty profit, while someone else looks after product development and order fulfillment.

Sounds like a pretty great deal, right? Well, it can be. But there are advantages *and* disadvantages to this business model that you should know about before getting started. So keep reading and I'll explain what you need to do to steer clear of the scam artists and identify great partners who will ship brand-name products on your behalf and help you generate sales without taking you to the cleaners.

How Drop Shipping Works

Let's say Mary sets up a Web site where she sells a product called "The Total Skin Care Package," priced at $97. A customer visits her site, places an order, and is billed $97 plus $11 for shipping and handling.

Mary then sends her distributor e-mail with her customer's order and shipping information. The manufacturer packs up the customer's order, puts Mary's shipping label on the package, and mails it out via UPS or FedEx, usually within 48 hours.

The distributor then bills Mary for the wholesale price of the "Total Skin Care Package"—in this case, $64 plus $11 for shipping and handling. Since Mary has passed the shipping and handling fee on to her customer, she just netted a profit of $33. And all she had to do was send her manufacturer e-mail!

Drop Shipping Advantages

In addition to not having to worry about shipping products, there are a few other advantages to this business model. First, it saves you the cost of building your own inventory. If you're like most people starting a small business, you don't have a ton of extra money lying around—the last thing you want to do is tie up your cash in inventory that you may or may not be able to sell.

Second, no inventory also means no leftovers. If the product you sell suddenly becomes outdated, obsolete or just plain untrendy, you aren't the one with a room or warehouse full of stock nobody will buy. Many online retailers find themselves having to offer deep discounts—and taking huge losses—on old products just to get them out of their homes or warehouses to make room for more inventories.

Third, you'll be able to add new products to your site almost instantly. Since you don't have to worry about stocking inventory, if you find that your customers are clamoring for a particular product, it's not unrealistic to expect you could add the item to your site in just a few days.

Choosing Your Drop Shipper

So how do you go about finding a reputable drop shipper for your business? Well, here's where doing your homework pays off. Whenever possible, you'll want to set up drop shipping arrangements directly with the manufacturers of the products you want to sell. The fewer middlemen you have to go through, the bigger your profits will be.

If, after contacting the manufacturer, they agree to drop ship for you, great! You can be confident they'll offer you a competitive price. If they don't agree to drop ship for you, you'll have to look for another alternative.

This usually means tracking down a distributor. A distributor is simply a company that maintains a large inventory of another company's products and distributes those products to smaller companies. The best way to locate a distributor is to simply ask the manufacturer of the product to recommend one.

Another great way to find a distributor for the type of product you wish to sell is by looking through related trade magazines. You'll frequently find manufacturers and distributors advertised in the backs of these publications. To find appropriate trade magazines, check out SmallBusiness101 and Yahoo's listing of trade magazines (see link in Appendix). Plus, you may also be able to find distributors and manufacturers using the Thomas Register. They provide listings for thousands of companies broken down by product, brand name and company name.

Most companies you contact will be more than happy to speak with you—after all, you're going to be selling their products for them. When you call, simply ask to speak with someone about becoming a vendor for his or her products. Once the switchboard puts you through to the right person, they'll be able to answer any questions you have, including:

1. What is the wholesale price they can offer you on their products? You'll need to make sure the wholesale price they offer is low enough that you'll be able to generate a good profit based on what you will be able to sell their products for.

2. Do they charge a handling fee for drop shipping? If so, how much? Most companies that drop ship will simply add the cost of UPS or FedEx shipping onto your wholesale price, but some will also charge you a handling fee (generally between $1 and $5). This is to offset their cost of picking, packing, and processing the order for you.

3. How do they ship their products? Almost every company that drop ships products will use a major nationwide delivery service like UPS or FedEx. Ask them to include tracking numbers with the order confirmations they send. This will save you many potential problems when customers ask, "Where is my order?"

4. How do they bill you? Most drop shippers will bill your credit card the wholesale price of the product plus shipping and handling as soon as they receive an order from you. With others, you may be able to set up a monthly billing cycle where you submit payment for all orders at the end of each month.

5. How do they deal with product returns? Be sure to find out what their policy is regarding returns. Most reputable companies will offer some kind of guarantee or warranty on their products and will deal with returns for you. This way, if a customer contacts you with a return, you can simply tell them the manufacturer will be happy to speak with them directly. If your manufacturer doesn't accept returns, look out! You'll be the one stuck replacing defective merchandise for your customers.

The fact is there are a lot of people making excellent full-time incomes—even six-figure incomes—with drop shipping. However, there is also no shortage of crooks and scam artists just waiting to take your money in exchange for the promise of "Instant Drop Shipping Riches" or "Ready-Made Online Drop Shipping Stores."

So here are a few things to watch out for when you're researching drop shipping:

- **Companies offering to sell you lists of drop shippers for $3, $4, and $7.** The old saying "You get what you pay for" applies here. Spend $4 on a drop-shipping list, and you'll get an e-mail listing 200 company names, addresses and maybe phone numbers. A few calls to out-of-service numbers, and you'll realize that the list is years old and basically useless.

- **Companies charging you a "monthly fee" to be your drop shipper.** Think about it: Why would a company charge you to sell you things? Answer: Because their products are either worthless junk or they're marked up way too high. In either case, they know your online store won't be able to sell any of them, so they need to make their money from you through a monthly fee.

- **Companies offering you a turnkey online business, complete with Web site, products that can only be purchased from them), and a merchant account that allows you to accept credit cards.** The strategy here is to get you to spend *your* money advertising and selling their products that they're buying from *real* wholesalers, marking up and selling to you. These companies usually also charge a one-time and/or monthly fee.

Here's the bottom line: No one's going to do your work for you. If you want to set up a real online business, you're going to need to do some legwork. Always look twice at any company that offers to make your job "easier" by giving you lists of hyped products to sell or offers to set up your site for "free"—chances are, their "all-in-one" solution will eat up a hefty portion of your profits.

Final Thoughts

Drop shipping can be an easy way to get started selling online. Since the manufacturer or distributor takes care of warehousing and shipping, you'll be able to concentrate your efforts on building your site and marketing your products. And this is what most entrepreneurs are good at.

When searching for a product to drop ship, don't spend money on "drop shipping directories." Think about it: Not only is their information frequently out of date, but everyone who buys these lists will be contacting the same companies, which means more competition for the products you'll be selling.

And choose your products carefully:

1. Make sure there aren't already hundreds of sites selling the same thing at prices you can't afford to compete with.

2. Choose products that target a "niche" market rather than "everyone." You'll always be more successful with this strategy.

3. Ask yourself: Is this a product I would buy myself?

Most important, remember that drop shipping isn't a magic formula that will make you rich. Building a business always takes a certain amount of hard work. The real "magic" is that drop shipping allows you to invest your money in marketing rather than inventory, and a well-planned marketing strategy is what will ultimately help you build a lucrative online income.

There are directories that cover over a half million products, from more than a thousand well-known brand names. So why does everyone who uses the directories try to sell electronics, for example?

Ok, I guess I did the same thing," says Chris Malta, one of the most successful businessmen on the Internet. "When I opened my first Internet store, I plastered the walls of that place with things that I though was cool. Stereo equipment, DVD players, Computer components. The shinier the better. I had the latest technology up there. Some of the items cost thousands of dollars. I think that in the back of my mind, I knew that I wasn't going to sell much of it, but it LOOKED cool. I could show it to my friends and say, "Check it out…that's MY store!" They were all suitably impressed, and I could walk around feeling like I was pretty slick. Whenever any of them asked me how much money I was making, I cleverly changed the subject."

The truth was that no one was buying much. Come to think of it, none of his friends bought anything, either. That should have told him something right there.

Electronics are a fine product to sell on the Internet. The problem is not the product; it's the COMPETITION.

Most of the people who start an Internet store want to know what the hottest sellers are on the 'Net, so they can sell those products too. They're missing the point, as Chris did. If you only sell the hottest sellers, you dilute your available customer base, because everyone else is trying to sell the hottest sellers! You also run into those bricks-and-mortar popular-item superstores that have millions of dollars to purchase tons of inventories at rock-bottom prices.

People buy all kinds of products. They don't have to be cool or shiny. *They just have to be things that people will buy.*

Here's an important ingredient for success on the 'Net: sell those products that people use, but don't stumble over every time they open a web browser.

When you build an Internet store, do a little research first. At eBay, you know that at least 90% of your traffic is going to come from the millions of people who surf through there with their purses and wallets flapping in the breeze. So, when you consider a new product line, you start a search.

If you were considering selling jewelry and watches, for example, you would do a search on the term "jewelry and watches" at eBay. As of the date this was written, such a search turned up over 91,000 items available…

Do you want to become store number 91,458, add 20 or 30 products to the nearly 8,000 that are already available, and hope you sell something?

I think not.

A Drop Ship distributor is a wholesale company that will ship one product at a time directly to your Internet customer for you, right from the warehouse.

Without Spending a CENT!
...Using Drop Ship Distributors

You don't pay up front to stock products. **You don't warehouse** anything, **or ship** anything. You simply place product information (images and descriptions) on your Internet site or auction, take orders, and email those orders to your Drop Ship distributor. THEY ship the product to your customer's door. You never have to touch it. YOU set your retail price, and pay the distributor the wholesale price, making **a profit every time.**

It's a great way to start an Internet business for **VERY little money.**

You have to be careful when looking for drop shippers. There are many scams out there as with anything else. People will take your money and not give you the help and knowledge you think you are buying. Be careful of tags such as "**Pro**", "**Global**", "**Millennium**", "**Bible**", "**Central**", "**Wholesalers**", etc. They are not telling you the whole truth.

WE tell you the *TRUTH*

Here's how a REAL Drop Ship distributor works:

- A REAL Drop Shipper is a factory-authorized wholesale distributor, or sometimes the actual manufacturer of their products. They ship to your customer from their OWN warehouse. NO middlemen or resellers cheating you out of your profits.

- A REAL Drop Shipper (with VERY FEW legitimate <u>exceptions</u>) will not charge you an "<u>account setup fee</u>".

- A REAL Drop Shipper will never force you to place a "minimum quantity order"; they will ship *one product at a time* to your customer with NO quantity commitments.

What's an "Account Setup Fee"

Real wholesale drop shippers do not charge you a setup fee to open an account for you.

When you do business with a genuine wholesale distributor, you contact them and open an "account". This is usually as simple as giving them your business name, address, and some other basic information. Then, they assign you an "account number", and you use that account number when you place orders with them.

However, there are a LOT of people on the Internet who want you to THINK that they are a real wholesaler.

Here's how it works:
- There are a tremendous number of people out there who act as **"middlemen"** in the drop shipping business.
- They set up **their own account** with a **real** drop shipper. Then they tell **YOU** that they **ARE** the real drop shipper, in order to rip you off.
- **They pretend to be an actual wholesale company**, with their own warehouse, shipping facilities, etc. They take your orders, then email those orders to the **real** drop shipper, and **charge you a profit on each order. They're taking you** for money you should not have to spend. They're getting in the **middle, between** you and the **real** drop shipper.
- **Here's the catch: they know that you're going to find out** that they are **not for real**, once you start doing business with them. Because of this, they will charge you an **account setup fee. That's all they really wanted from you in the first place…**that account setup fee! By the time you find out you're **dealing with a phony,**

they've got your account setup fee, and **you won't get it back.** If they happen to make a few bucks off your orders before you catch on, so much the better for them.

Note: We all know that there are exceptions to every rule!

There are a VERY few genuine drop ship wholesalers who DO charge a SMALL account setup fee (less than $40.00, for example), and it's legitimate. Some of these companies provide **extra services and value to your business, such as:**

- Custom shipping labels they may print for you.
- They may set you up with access to a special administrative area on their web site, where you can track your orders and shipments.
- They may set you up with real-time access to their database of available stock and "quantity on hand" of their products.

All these things cost the wholesaler money, so they may legitimately charge a fee to set up your account.

However, this is VERY rare! 98% of the "drop shippers" on the Internet who charge Account Setup Fees **ARE middlemen!**

<u>If you have come across</u> a "drop shipper" that charges any kind of fee to open your account, and you are **not sure it's legitimate,** refer to the Appendix section at the end of this book for an e-mail address should you have questions about whether a drop shipper is legitimate.

Don't throw your money away on cheap lists and sites full of middlemen, resellers and closeout liquidators that charge you overblown prices, <u>account setup fees</u> and minimums. **The creators of those lists and sites are irresponsible people** who couldn't care less what happens to you. **They pad their lists** with the names of hundreds, or even thousands of companies that are **USELESS to you, and they KNOW IT!** You'll waste valuable time and money finding out that the information you bought is virtually worthless.

Since you use the directory exclusively as a source of product suppliers who drop ship, you go back to the Directory and look around at some of the available product types. You notice that one of the wholesalers you list carries "XYZ" brand Yard and Garden tools. Will people buy these products? Hmmm…people HAVE been known to work on their yards and gardens, when they're not playing with their electronics. "XYZ" (example only!) is a well-known brand name, so our customers would feel comfortable with it.

So let's check out the competition.

You want to know how many other people are selling "XYZ" products in the Internet Mall where our store is visible. So you search on "XYZ". Only 54 stores selling "XYZ products! That's considerably better than 497 stores selling the electronics you were considering.

Are these stores devoted to selling ONLY "XYZ" products? Wow…not even one! All the top search returns are stores selling general merchandise.

When you build a store, you like to specialize in one product line. There are many benefits to this; chiefly the fact that customers feel more comfortable in a store that does one thing, and does it well. It's also much easier to rank a single product line in the major search engines than it is to rank a general store with lots of unrelated products.

Ok, you have a product line that you feel will sell, and the competition in the "XYZ" brand name itself is minimal and unfocused.

However, when people search for garden tools, they're going to use search words like "Trowel", and "Pruning". They're not going to search on the term "XYZ" very often. So, you go back to the Internet Mall search engine.

You search on "Gardening Tools", and you find 113 stores carrying 324 products. Still not much competition. Even better, NONE of these stores are focused on just gardening tools. They are gift stores, general merchandise stores, etc., who just happen to have the word "Gardening" somewhere in their product description. You know that you can put the word "Gardening" in our very product names themselves (ex.—"Gardening Trowel, Steel, 9 Inch"), and you will show up right near the TOP of a search on the word "Gardening".

You search on the word "Pruning", and find 81 stores carrying 418 products. Still not a problem, since the top returns are BOOKS on pruning, and the rest are more unfocused sites.

After a little more searching, you're convinced that you've found a product line that will sell well for the Spring and Summer seasons. In the Fall, sales will slack off, but you have other stores that are geared toward Fall and Winter merchandise. They are also small and focused, and no matter how many eBay Stores you open, you know that each one of them will easily cover it's monthly cost, and turn a profit of some kind all year 'round.

Finding a drop shipper who is reputable will take some research and time. The American Drop Shippers Directory is only $15.00 at their site. (URL's are noted in the appendix section). This is a very reasonable price as many other directories sell for upwards of $50.00.

The appendix provides a directory of wholesale distributors. Please always keep in mind what has been said before:

✓ **BE CAREFUL** of the scams.

✓ **DO NOT** fall for big account set up fees

✓ **BE SURE** they are legitimate! Use the e-mail address provided in the appendix section at the end of this book to find out.

✓ **MAKE SURE** there are no middlemen that add on their own markup.

Drop shipping can make a lot of money on eBay if you find a niche that has not been saturated. Go through the list of wholesale distributors and find one or two that sell the type of item you are interested in.

Research them thoroughly! Take your time. Look for distributors that will sell in small quantities as well as large. You don't want to fill your garage with items that may never sell. So make sure they will drop ship to your customers. This research will take plenty of time to weed out the ones you feel comfortable with. It is worth every second of that time to ensure you are dealing with honest wholesalers.

The idea is not to fill up your home with a lot of goods. You need to find a distributor who will send the item directly to the buyer without you having to stock the items. Also, be sure of their payment methods. **ASK QUESTIONS!**

HALF BAY.com

Half.com was recently bought out by eBay adding to its already profitable business a way to sell your unwanted items for cash. Everything here is used.

Do you love finding great deals? Have you ever wanted an easy way to turn your stuff into cash? If you answered 'yes' to either (or both) of these questions then Half.com is the perfect place for you!

Half.com is an innovative online marketplace that brings together buyers and sellers just like you. Although Half.com is part of eBay, it is not an auction. There is no bidding or waiting around to see if you have the winning bid. Everything is available for immediate purchase at incredibly discounted prices and listing items for sale is FREE. From books and baseball gloves to computers and CDs, Half.com is the perfect marketplace for all sorts of fantastic stuff.

Selling—How does it work?

Half.com is the place for you to turn your unwanted stuff into cash. Here, you can sell all sorts of stuff, like books, CDs, movies, video games, home electronics, computer equipment, trading cards, sporting goods, etc.

Listing your stuff for sale is easy on Half.com. In many cases, Half.com's catalog already contains all the information that buyers are looking for on the product you're listing for sale. However, if you are listing an item that is not a book, CD, movie or video game and the item is not in our catalog we'll provide you with the tools needed to get it listed.

Best of all, listing items for sale is **FREE** at Half.com. Once you list your stuff, it's almost as simple as watching the money roll in. Here's how to do it, in 3 easy steps:

Selling—How does it work?

Half.com is the place for you to turn your unwanted stuff into cash. Here, you can sell all sorts of stuff, like books, CDs, movies, video games, home electronics, computer equipment, trading cards, sporting goods, etc. Listing your stuff for sale is easy on Half.com. In many cases, Half.com's catalog already contains all the information that buyers are looking for on the product you're listing for sale. However, if you are listing an item that is not a book, CD, movie or video game and the item is not in our catalog we'll provide you with the tools needed to get it listed.

Best of all, listing items for sale is **FREE** at Half.com. Once you list your stuff, it's almost as simple as watching the money roll in. Here's how to do it, in 3 easy steps:

SELL YOUR STUFF!

Click 'Sell Your Stuff' at the top of any page and enter the appropriate item 'number' (for example, ISBN for books or UPC code for CDs, movies, electronics, etc.) to find the item. You can also run a search from any page to find the particular item you wish to sell. On the item's detail page click on the 'Sell Yours Now' button to begin listing it for sale.

Looking to list a lot of items for sale?

If you have a lot of items to sell click on the "Find out what we can do for you" link on the 'Start Selling' page to find out how Half.com can help you list a lot of items at once.

Can't find your item in our catalog?

If you are selling items outside of books, CDs, movies and games and you can't find the item you want to sell in our catalog, Half.com will help you describe the item to us by asking you some basic questions. Simply tell us what you know about the item and we'll help you list it.

Step Two

When you are listing items for sale, use our quality ratings to describe the condition of your item and type in a short note (e.g. "Still in shrink-wrap", "Human bite marks on cover", etc.). Click 'Continue'. Next, pick a price, select your shipping method (if you haven't already determined it in your account), click 'Add Item' and you're in business! For items outside the books, music, movies and games categories, you can also add a 1000 word description and upload a picture of the item.

Step Three

As soon as someone's bought one of your items, we'll send you an email. All you need to do is a.) reply to the email so we know you'll be sending the item in the next 24 hours and b.) package it up well so the item is protected and ship it.

How do I get paid for my sales?

You can either get paid via Direct Deposit or paper check. Payments via Direct

Deposit will be paid twice monthly. Payment periods will end on the 15th and last day of each month. Your seller balance at the end of each period will be deposited in your personal checking account within 7 business days from the end of the period. Payments via check will be made up to twice a month, depending on how much you sell.

Your payments will be for the amount you've sold minus a 15% commission. Half.com will pay a fixed shipping reimbursement for all sales in their book, music, movie and video game product categories. For all other categories, there is no shipping reimbursement, however they allow you to enter a shipping amount as part of your overall item price.

Half.com is safe and secure. Your credit card information is encrypted using SSL, and no one else ever sees it. When you make a purchase, we charge your credit card, making Half.com safe and convenient. They will never give out your personal information, or your e-mail. This method of selling is easy without all of the set up and rules with eBay. However, it's only for those unwanted items you have around the house. People also buy items at garage sales and second hand stores to sell at Half.com.

You have read all of the information contained in this book. Now you are ready to venture into your online business. What an exciting time of life this is! The world is at your feet, and your confidence is high. You know the possibilities are endless. Believe in yourself and you **will** be successful.

In A Nutshell

To sum it all up, this is your business. You will spend the next few months thinking, planning, researching and creating your very own eBay business with the goal of making money. Your attitude must be positive.

Do not listen to negative people. If you can dream it up, you can do it. Take your time choosing products. Do your homework. Don't get discouraged. Failures are the best teacher and getting up to try again is a sign of a true entrepreneur. Here are a few more reminders for you.

Never break your promises.

If you say, "I will email you back with that information today," or "We will ship that out to you within 24 hours," then DO IT. Make a promise once to a customer and then break it, and they will think, "Oh, too bad, this business has poor customer service just like every other business..." Continually breaking your promises to customers will earn your business a reputation as flaky and unreliable-and, guess what? you will lose your customers. If you can't keep a promise, then don't make it; if you do make a promise, then also make every possible effort to keep it. Period

Forget that your customers have a strong sense of fair play.

You need to make sure that you always treat them fairly, first come-first served; fair pricing and shipping charges; fair policies-because if you don't treat them fairly, they will find out about it and leave you. For example, a friend of mine ordered something from an online shopping site that was listed as "in stock." A couple of months later, he received an email from them saying that the item was actually out of stock when he ordered it and that they were, once again, out of stock. The kicker is, the site had the item in stock several times between when my friend ordered it and when they notified him-but because when he ordered it was out of stock, they never sent the order! However, other people obviously ordered and received the item in the same period of time that he was waiting for it. Then when he called them, they said, in essence, "Sorry, we can't help you." My friend will never order anything from that site again-they violated basic rules of fairness in dealing with him. Don't let this kind of stuff drive your customers away; if there are flaws in your system that have the potential to cause unfairness, start fixing them now.

Never Forget to say "thank you."

A web developer that I know has a system for working with clients in which he says "thank you" (in letters, cards, lunches, and flowers) no less than seven times over the course of his relationship with the client-from the first contact to the maintenance contract. He's very successful doing this. Make it a point to say, "thank you" at every opportunity-your customers will feel like you really appreciate and value them.

Treat every customer like a completely precious individual. Relate to him or her as if they were the only person in the world, while you're on the phone, in chat, or writing an email to them. Customers love personal attention, so hang on their every word and don't let yourself get interrupted. Remember that your customers are absolutely the lifeblood of your business, and treat them accordingly. No, I'm not suggesting that you form romantic attachments with your customers! But they will sense whether you believe they are valuable. So you must believe that they are valuable and then put that belief into action.

When you list items to sell be aware that they will close at that exact time 3, 5, or 9 days later, depending on how many days you choose.

+

Lots of savvy shoppers will wait until an item is closing and then zap in a bid, knowing that they will probably get what they want without having to enter into a bidding war.

=

Even if you are a night owl, at your peak at 3 a.m., that is not the best time to list your items for sale unless you are selling something that only other night owls would want. (Feathers?)

You may be saying, "What is she talking about?"

Decide what to sell. In my opinion, the hardest element of selling on eBay is deciding what to sell. If you are lucky, you have wholesale access to something that a lot of people use. I only have one piece of advice about this. Research. If you have an idea see if others are selling it and for how much. Search the Internet for wholesale purchases, but be wary: Just because something is advertised as wholesale doesn't mean it really is. Get a tax ID number from your state so that you can purchase wholesale. Be aware that most wholesale operations require you to purchase things in lots. 100 pieces of the same toy may work in a retail store, but it can take you a long, long time to sell them one at a time on eBay.

Identify the audience. If you are selling things that new mothers might be interested in, think about what times of day or night they might most logically have time to actually sit down at a computer and shop. If you are selling things that someone might want in their office it might be best to make sure the auction closes after traditional work hours.

Think about the difference in the time zones. I have the best luck if I calculate things based on the Central time zone. That way I can catch people from both coasts as well. Consider a strategy you might use to sell Vermont syrup. My guess would be that you would have more potential customers the greater distances from Vermont where it is not readily available. So time your auction closing for people living on the west coast or the deep south or in other countries. Don't hesitate to start auctions at several different times if you have multiple similar items to sell.

Understand the importance of eBay's rating system. It is extremely important. Your rating of positive and negative points is the only way you have to assure potential buyers that you are honest and reliable. If someone gives you a negative rating don't respond to it while you are angry. There comments and your response will be there forever. I once gave someone a negative because they did not pay despite numerous requests. The buyer then gave me a negative, noting that I only gave him a month to pay. I didn't have to respond to that comment. He did himself in because all eBayers know that payment is to be received within 10 days of the close of an auction. Anyone can go into your record and read every comment that has been written from the day you started buying or selling. A couple of negatives like the one above are not going to hurt your rating in the long run and non payers need to get negative ratings because the seller has to pay the eBay fees even if the sale doesn't go through. However, it is in your best interest to make sure you have made every effort to collect. Sometimes things get lost, people forget or get sick, and sometimes houses burn down.

Also important to the rating system is the need to be very careful that you give an accurate description of any item you are selling, including listing any flaws that might exist. If you are selling an expensive, brand name, handbag it is very important that you check the inside tag to see if it has been clipped or not. Clipping means the item is a second and it will not sell for as much as an item with in intact tag. If you don't include that information, you will probably earn a bad reputation. If you are unsure about what is, or is not, important read other ads for similar items and see what information reoccurs from ad to ad.

Don't list multiples at the same time in the same category. Savvy shoppers will always check to see if there is more than one listing, and, savvy shoppers frequently shop by item name. For instance, I might run a search for Macintosh memory. No matter what category the seller has chosen for the listing, if it has the words Macintosh and memory in the title it will show up in my request list. It would not take me more than a few minutes to discover that seller A has 6 listings for the exact same kind of memory. If the first 3 have bids already in place, I will go to one of the last 3 listings, hoping that no one will bid against me, raising the price. If you are selling something that you can reasonably expect bidders to fight over, wait until one sells before listing another.

A Picture Says A Thousand Words

Will a picture sell it? Sellers need to also consider how well their items can be described in a picture. Your rating, the price, and the picture are the combination of things that can win or loose a sale. If you are selling something small like a book, scan the book jacket for your image. Everything will be easy to see in the resulting picture. Other things require traditional pictures. Anything black is going to be hard to show adequately. Think about the background, and if the item is two pieces, take two pictures. Also, consider advertisement pictures that you may have available. A lot of people selling Pottery Barn items keep old catalogues and if they find something they want to sell, they look back through the catalogues and scan in the catalogue picture. Mind the copyright of any images you may use, however.

It is also very important to reduce your picture so that the file size is as small as possible, while still presenting a viewable image. Remember that not everyone has a fast computer or a fast Internet connection. If your picture takes too long to download, many shoppers will just skip to the next auction. With the Internet downloads, patience is not a virtue.

The Gallery

When listing your auction you will have the option of choosing a "gallery" listing. This is a small version of the image you have included in your ad. It shows up to the left of your listing on listing pages and at the top left of your specific auction page. Gallery listings cost US$.25. A potential bidder may be looking for a red shirt. If the bidder does a search for men's casual shirts in size L he or she may get 1,500 listings. It is not uncommon for the potential bidder to simply scroll down the pages, and quickly glancing at the gallery images for anything red. Those will probably be the only auctions that the bidder opens.

Start Me Up

What should be the starting bid? This is a biggie because you pay a listing fee based on your starting minimum bid. So do you start at US$1.00 or do you start at the minimum you are willing to take? Like everything else in life, it depends. If you are selling something so popular that you know absolutely, positively that it will sell for at least a specific price, then it will probably be safe to start the bidding at a low amount. However, and this is a big however, if you list something for US$1.00 and you only get one bid, you will have to sell the item for US$1.00.

Unless, of course, you have set a reserve price on your auction. A reserve price indicates a minimum price below which you will not sell the item. The problem with this is that the bidder will not know what that reserve price is, and that can make some bidders angry. However, selecting a reserve option means that you can list the item starting at a low amount without taking any chances on not getting what the item is worth. If you think this option is for you, I suggest you read all the details at eBay before using it.

It is in your best interest as a seller to ship as inexpensively as possible while getting it delivered as quickly as possible, but this is going to depend somewhat on what is easiest for you.

My recommendation for new sellers in the US is to use Priority Mail with the US Postal Service. The mailing supplies are free and bidders are accustomed to paying for priority delivery. Keep in mind that the post office has changed how rates are calculated. If your package is under 1 pound, the rate will be $3.85 anywhere in the U.S. Above 1 pound the fees depend on the postal zone (Zip Code). eBay has recently started including the winners Zip Code along with the auction sold message, which makes it easy for you to calculate the correct rate.

If you have the means to weigh your package you can quickly go to the USPS Web site and calculate the exact postage amount to send to the winner. The domestic postage calculator can be found here. There is also an international postage calculator available at the same web site.

Wrap It Up

Finally, I suggest you include some kind of documentation with your package that summarizes the details of the sale, including the auction number. Even a copy of e-mail or the ad itself will suffice. If you want to look really professional, create an invoice, or purchase software that will create them for you. You need some kind of record for taxes no matter what method you use.

How much does it weigh? Before you choose to sell something on eBay consider how much it will cost to ship it to the buyer. Buyers almost always pay shipping so shipping fees are important as they decide whether to bid or not. If I can get a good deal on a new Mac I probably won't mind spending $60 to have it shipped to me. However, I am not going to bid on an item if the shipping will be more than the item is worth. I will be much more inclined to purchase what I need at a local store.

Include Brand names. You might be surprised how many people shop by brand name. If you don't believe me do a search for Pottery Barn. At any given time you will find more than 1,000 items listed, all of which include the Pottery Barn name in the title. Also, where relevant, include sizes in the title. Many shoppers, looking for clothes, search by size because otherwise the listings are overwhelming.

MORE HINTS

NEWSGROUPS

There are thousands of Newsgroups on the Internet, covering every conceivable subject. The first thing to do is to download the names of all of them. Your e-mail program will be able to do this for you very easily. If you use Microsoft Outlook Express then go to Tools and Newsgroups. You'll then be prompted to download the complete list. This will probably take around 15 minutes, depending on how fast or slow your connection is.

When you have the full list (which can vary slightly according to which ISP you use, but generally they all give access to the same Newsgroups) you should be able to do a search to select those that are connected with the business you are in. You can then choose to subscribe to some or all of them.

Having selected those Newsgroups that would be useful in promoting your business, go online and download the messages currently posted to each one. Your e-mail program is probably set at a default of downloading around 300 headers at a time. You can set this as low as 50 if you don't want to spend time reading through hundreds of messages at each Newsgroup you've subscribed to.

When the headers have downloaded select the messages you want to download by clicking on the appropriate heading. Some messages can be very long, so keep an eye on the size of each message in kilobytes before clicking on it. When you've downloaded all the messages you're interested in from each Newsgroup, you can come offline to view them.

It's usual to lurk in Newsgroups before posting to them. This means simply that you read through a good number of messages posted by other members of the Newsgroup before posting anything yourself. This is so that you can note the various rules and etiquette relating to that Newsgroup. Otherwise, you risk annoying other members, particularly if you post an ad for your business in a Newsgroup that does not normally carry ads, and you might get flamed. Some Newsgroups have a moderator who reviews all messages submitted to it to ensure they are suitable. These Newsgroups usually have the word moderated in their name.

Once you are familiar with your chosen Newsgroups, you can start posting to them. Often it's not a good idea to actually post a brazen advert for your business, but better to join in or start a conversation thread in which you can mention your business, or simply put your signature (in which you doubtless mention your business website address) at the foot of each message. Other Newsgroups are little more than a posting board for various ads, often for get rich quick schemes.

One of the best things about Newsgroups is that they are all free. The downside is that as a result the business-oriented groups have messages posted to them continually, and when you post your message it will soon be buried in the mass of postings that come after yours. So you have to make your message stand out from the rest, and this takes quite a lot of practice.

Don't try to sell your product directly—most people reading the messages are looking for something for nothing. Try to get people to your website, which doubtless will have a terrific sales message on it :-), or put in the e-mail address of an auto responder and invite them to click for further information.

Don't spend too much time on the Newsgroups, but posting regularly can give you a steady trickle of business.

CLASSIFIED AD SITES

These abound all over the Internet. The leading Search Engines usually have a section of classifieds, and many of them are free. Because of this, the same drawbacks apply as do to the Newsgroups, so don't spend too much time on them or expect very much business. But it's still often worth posting classifieds. Do a search for "free classified ads" and you will get more results than you know what to do with.

To really succeed with classified ads, you have to practice writing both headlines and copy. And the golden rule is to test, test and test some more. When you have an ad that returns a good response, after a while you may want to change the headline or the body. Only change one thing at a time, so you can constantly monitor the results. That way, if the change leads to a reduction in response then you can quickly and easily cancel it and revert to what the ad was before. If it results in an improvement, you can incorporate the change and then make another single change to see if that further improves or diminishes the response.

The most successful entrepreneurs are constantly testing their ads, seeking improvement. Of course, to do this you need to key each ad, so you can trace each response to a specific ad, and keep track of each ad's performance. Do this by varying the e-mail address to respond to, or the heading of the e-mail, which you can control by inserting, e.g. ?subject=adcode1 after the e-mail address.

Choose a good top-level domain name.

As a business owner, you need a top-level domain, e.g. www.yourname.com. A sub domain, such as www.serviceprovider.com/freepages/yourname just won't impress anybody and will lose you much more money than you'd save. Check and see if the name you want is still available by visiting www.register.com or www.webnic.registrars.com. If it is available, register it quickly. The price of .com names has fallen sharply and is no more than about $12, sometimes less, depending on whom you buy it through.

Your name or your company name is not necessarily the best domain name for you. Consider registering a descriptive name based on what business, you are in. For example, a real estate agent specializing in selling holiday homes in Florida might call itself www.floridahomes.com. I haven't checked, but that domain name is almost certainly taken. You can probably think of a name that would aptly describe your business, or the commodity you deal in. That is the best name for your web site, particularly if it comprises the word or words that a potential customer might typically enter into a search engine to find the goods or services that you supply.

APPENDIX OF RESOURCES

Links for drop shipper catalogs:

www.bookservices.com

Item # 2085516988 at eBay: put this number in the search box. This book of wholesale distributors is only $2.99.

Chris Malta—one of the most well known experts on drop shipping:

http://198.65.239.163/main/StartingYourBusiness.html

The eBay Marketer:

http://www.ebaymarketer.com/Download/thankyou.cfm

eBay Exposed Newsletter

www.ebayexposed.com

Nancy Carroll Gravely—The Mac Observer

Corey Rudl, president of Internet Marketing Center, *is the author of* Insider Secrets to Marketing Your Business on the Internet, *a comprehensive how-to guide for e-business success, which reveals strategies for generating traffic, increasing revenues and automating your online businesses. Contact* ques-tions@marketingtips.com *for free tips and resources.*

List of Wholesale Distributors:

ABC Discount Company
2829 Main Street
Jacksonville, FL 32206
Phone#: 904-356-4121
http://www.uniformscrubs4less.com

ABC Import & Export Co
2 Gourmet Ln
Edison, NJ 08817

ABCO International
Phone#: 407-896-6000

AB Distribution
Phone#: 908-284-1780

ACL Inc.
2155 Bering Drive
San Jose, CA 95131
Phone#: 800-888-0348

Accessories Palace Inc.
Phone# 561-582-1812
http://www.wholesalecentral.com/accessoriespalace

ACI
173 2nd Ave
Brooklyn, NY 11215
Phone#: 800-847-8053

Acusport Corp.
1 Hunter Place
Bellfontaine, OH 43311
Phone#: 800-543-3150

A Discount Warehouse, Inc.
10092 NW 53rd St.
Sunrise, FL 33351
Phone#: 954-746-8701
http://www.closeouts.digiscape.net

Admor Memory Corp.
217 Technolgy Drive Bldg #100
Irvine, CA 92618
http://www.admor.com

Advanced Design
300 Seaboard Ave
Venice, FL 34292
Phone#: 800-832-5221
Advanced PCBoost
http://www.pcboost.com

Agcity—

Home based opportunities in wholesaling

www.agcitybooks.com/

Alamo Outlet
39 S. Court
Alamo, TN 38001
Phone#: 901-696-5151

All Right Sales
4201-03 N. Kedzie Ave
Chicago, IL 60618

Allstar Enterprises Inc.
51 Stouts Lane Suite 1
Monmouth Junction, NJ 08852
Phone# 908-329-6095
Fax# 908-329-6238

American Design Group
9835 Manchester Road
St. Louis, MO 63119
Phone#: 800-456-6886

American Indian Fashions
2407 E. Boyd Ave Ste 11B
Gallup, NM 87301-7411
Phone#: 505-722-6837

American Merchandise Liquidators, Inc.
15810-A Highway 59
Foley, AL 36535
Phone#: 334-970-1100
http://www.amlinc.com

American Rod & Gun
PO Box 2820
Springfield, MO 65801
Phone#: 800-332-5377
http://www.ar-g.com

America's Liquidators
624 Lake Shore Dr.
Maitland, FL 32751
Phone# 407-814-8700

Amish Folk Remedies
27539 W. Londick
Burr Oak, MI 49030

Amtrat International Corporation
34015 Seventh Street
Union City, CA 94587
Phone#: 510-476-0500
http://www.amtrat.com

Andron Division
30 Center Road
Palmetto, FL 06033
Phone#: 941-722-8202
http://www.towels.net

Angel Graphics
PO Box 530
Fairfield, IA 52556
Phone#: 515-472-5481
Fax# 515-472-7353

Apparel Xprex Imports—Appollo Caps & Novelties
1184 Bonham Ave
Columbus, OH 43211
Phone#: 614-297-8899

Art-Mart
1601 Memorial Blvd.
Murfreesboro, TN 37129
Phone#: 615-890-1889
http://www.surplus.net/art-mart

Artmatic Cosmetics
4014 1st Ave
Brooklyn, NY 11232

Atco Corp.
216 Tosca Drive
Stoughton, MA 02072
Phone#: 800-969-2826

Atlantic Cable International
340 Garden Oaks Blvd.
Houston, TX 77018
Phone#: 800-245-5660
http://www.acicable.com

Atlantic Connection
Phone#: 614-766-0699
http://www.discounttrade.com

Atlantic Surplus Liquidators
214 Appledown Drive
Cary, NC 27513
Phone#: 919-462-1774

Atlantic Wholesale Inc.
5706-K General Washington Drive
Alexandria, VA 22312
Phone# 800-803-9815
http://www.wholesalewebdirect.com

Atlas Trading Ltd.
Phone#: 702-331-4077
http://www.surplus.net/atlas/

Austin Memory Inc.
7950 Anderson Square Suite 103
Austin, TX 78757
Phone#: 512-451-6667

B Listings
A B C D E F G H I J K L M N O P Q R S T U V W X Y Z

Backstage Fashion
PO Box 437
Sedona, AZ 86339
Phone#: 800-644-7625
http://www.wholesalecentral.com/backstagefashion

Badger Shooters Supply Inc.
202 N. Harding Street
Owen, WI 54460
Phone#: 800-424-9069

Banian Trading Co.
2252 Main Street Suite #9
Chula Vista, CA 91911
Phone#: 619-423-9975

Bass Pro
1935 S. Campbell
Springfield, MO 65898
Phone#: 800-227-7776
http://www.basspro.com

Batter's Choice
Phone#: 800-335-6169
http://www.batterschoice.com

Bedrock Gem & Stone
Phone#: 800-923-5044
http://www.wholesalewebdirect.com

Berg Enterprises
RR #1 Box 6320
Corinna, ME 04928
Phone#: 800242-2374

Best In Town
PO Box 58
Marlboro, NY 12542
Phone#: 914-236-4461

Better House Corp
1245 Broadway
Brooklyn, NY 11221
Phone#: 800-562-1311
http://www.wholesalewebdirect.com

Bill Wilson
Phone#: 319-391-1240

Boris Jewelry
624 Prospect Ave
Cleveland, OH 44115
Phone#: 216-771-7141
http://www.borisjewelers.com

Boyette & Associates
PO Box 1712
Brandon, MS 39043-1712

Brand Name Liquidators
Phone#: 706-277-1009
http://www.savehere.com

Buckiye HBB
Phone#: 937-275-6655

Business Advertising Specialties Corp
9351 De Soto Ave
Chatsworth, CA 91311

C Listings
A B C D E F G H I J K L M N O P Q R S T U V W X Y Z

California Time
121 W. Pico Blvd.
Los Angeles, CA 90015

Campbell Mcgrath Importers
South Ave and Hale St.
Cranford, NJ 07016

Can Tex USA
Phone#: 561-533-0495
http://www.cantek.com

Cardinal Inc./Dynasty Dolls
PO Box 99
400 Markley St.
Port Reading, NJ 07064

Cars N Trucks
18801 Thornwood Circle
Huntington Beach, CA 92646
Phone#: 888-888-9113
http://www.cars-n-trucks.com

CDW Computer Centers, Inc.
2840 Maria Ave
Northbrook, IL 60062-2026
Phone#: 800-800-4CDW

Charbeths Merchandise Corp
931-C Conklin St.
Farmington, NY 11735

Charles L. Adams Medicine Co.
4890 Clark Lane
Manlius, NY 13104

Cheap Bobs
Box 11223
1425 Tomoka Farms Rd.
Daytona Beach, FL 32120

Chicago Import Inc.
3333 W. Montrose Ave.
Chicago, IL 60618
Phone# 800-854-0881
Fax# 312-588-3285
http://www.wholesalewebdirect.com

Chico Arts
1045 Humble Place
El Paso, TX 79915
Phone#: 915-779-5636

Chiron Inc.
P.O. Box 365 Cote t Luc
Quebec, Canada, H4B2Y5
Phone# 541-597-9889
http://www.surplus.net/chiron

Cigars
Cigars, humidors, women's cigars
www.humidorguide.com

Chocolates ElRay
Gourmet chocolates
www.chocolates-elrey.com/chocolate_wholesale_distributor

C & J Dickinson
PO Box 3
Duvall, WA 98019
Phone#: 425-788-7899

CJ's Extra Innings
400 W. Broad St.
Westfield, NJ 07090
Phone#: 800-392-7738
http://www.wholesalewebdirect.com

CJ's Wholesale Socks
504 N. Gault Ave
Ft. Payne, AL 35967
Phone#: 256-845-7986

Clamor Impex, Inc.
214 NE 1st St.

Miami, FL 33132
Phone# 305-379-1701
http://www.wholesalecentral.com/clamor/

Clean Air N. Earth Tech
2121 Ponce De Leon Tech
Ste. 522
Coral Gables, FL 33134-5222

C & L Distributors
24 Deer Park Dr.
East Longmeadow, MA 01028

Closeout Net
http://closeout.net

Closeouts 2000 Inc.
12 South Dixie Hwy
Lake Worth, FL 33460
Phone#: 561-586-7388
http://www.closeouts2000inc.com

Clothes-Out Factory, Inc
59-47 Fresh Meadow Lane
Flushing, NY 11365
Phone#: 718-357-4849

Coast to Coast Liquidating
Phone#: 561-461-6255

Coburn's Wholesale
14841 Whittram Ave

Fontana, CA 92335
Phone#: 800-553-4867

Colorado Closeouts, Inc.
4800 Washington Street
Denver, CO 80216
Phone#: 303-988-9270

Colossal Jewelry & Accessories, Inc.
406 N. Midland Ave., Dept MF
Saddle Brook, NJ 07663
Phone#: 800-252-4206
http://www.wholesalewebdirect.com

Computer Hardware Wholesale
Phone#: 516-697-8132

Computer Smiths
101 South Knoxville
Russelville, AZ 72801
Phone#: 800-615-0888
http://www.web-smiths.com

Computer Wharehouse
465 North University Ave
Provo, UT 84601
Phone#: 800-372-0121

Conklin Fashions
72 Main Street
Sidney, NY 13838
Phone#: 800-437-1161
http://www.wholesalejewelry.net

Corbell Imports
1535 S. Sepulveda Blvd.
Los Angeles, CA 90025

Costume Jewelry Dist., Inc.
8116 5th Avenue
Brooklyn, NY 11209
Phone#: 800-404-2600

Countryside Closeouts
1309 Ridgely Ave
Springfield, IL 62702
Phone#: 217-241-3785
http://www.countryside-closeouts.com

Creasy's Outdoor Sports
3434 Buck Mountain Rd
Roanoke, VA 24014
Phone#: 800-888-0852

Creative Group
Park 80 West Plaza 2
Saddle Brook, NJ 07662

Creed Enterprises
P.O. Box 905
Dept. W
Abilene, TX 79604

CS Goodfriend & Co
11 Riverdale Ave
Port Chester, NY 10573

Custom Foam Products
PO Box 804
Belton, TX 76513
Phone #: 800-234-5740
Fax #: 817-939-1322
http://www.wholesalewebdirect.com

CVC Specialties
4510 S. Boyle Ave
Los Angeles, CA 90058

D Listings

A B C D E F G H I J K L M N O P Q R S T U V W X Y Z

Dallas Micro Distributing
4901 Keller Springs Road Ste #111
Addison, TX 75248
Phone#: 972-818-5600

Details
110 E. 9th St.
Lobby 13
Los Angeles, CA 90079

Direct Marketing Company
P.O. Box 6623
Bloomington, TN 47407-6623
Phone# 812-335-1980

Discount Food Products
Rd #1 Box 487
Olyphant, PA 18447
Phone#: 717-254-9246
http://www.surplus.net/dfp

Discount Home Improvement Outlet
10034 W. Floirssant
St. Louis, MO 63136
Phone# 314-388-0303
Fax# 314-388-1703
http://www.surplus.net/dhi-outlet

D & J Manufacturing Inc.
Toledo, OH
Phone#: 800-671-8654
http://www.wholesalewebdirect.com

D & L Distributors
http://www.surplus.net/randl/

Dresses For Less
920 S. Elmora Ave
Elizabeth, NJ 07202
Phone#: 908-289-3997

E Listings
<u>A</u> <u>B</u> <u>C</u> <u>D</u> <u>E</u> <u>F</u> <u>G</u> H I <u>J</u> <u>K</u> <u>L</u> <u>M</u> <u>N</u> <u>O</u> <u>P</u> <u>Q</u> <u>R</u> <u>S</u> <u>T</u> <u>U</u> <u>V</u> <u>W</u> X Y Z

Eagle Liquidators Inc.
215 Pineda St. Unit 181
Longwood, FL 32750
Phone#: 407-830-8636
http://www.eagletrade.com

Eagle Spirit Production
218 Grove Street
Bangor, ME 04401
Phone# 207-942-3442
http://www.visionwork.com/eaglespirit/

East-West Trading Corp.
4809 N. Elston Ave
Chicago, IL 60630
Phone#: 773-481-7197
http://www.wholesalewebdirect.com
Educorp Computer Services
7434 Trade St.
San Diego, CA 92121-2410
Phone#: 800-843-9497

Edwards Closeouts Inc.
Phone#: 305-557-7098

Egghead Discount Software
PO Box 177
Liberty Lake, WA 99019-0177

Phone#: 800-EGGHEAD
http://www.egghead.com

EJ Silverbrooke
PO Box 10207
Columbia, MO 66205

Electronic Bargains
PO Box 1038
Brockton, MA 02403-1038

Electronic Computer Warehouse
Email: sales@ecwo.com

Elictrical Sales International
Phone#: 813-685-1933

EMS-Janko
Phone#: 800-981-2828
http://www.wholesalewebdirect.com

Epoch Sales Website
Phone#: 800-736-3762
http://www.epochsales.com

Estairr Display Products
PO Box 25813
Anaheim, CA 92825

Evergreen Associates, Inc.
Phone# 847-587-9243
http://www.surplus.net/evergreen/

F Listings

A B C D E F G H I J K L M N O P Q R S T U V W X Y Z

Fallah Ent.
11601 Seaboard Circle
Stanton, CA 90680
Phone#: 714-379-6760
http://www.wholesalecentral.com/fallah

F.A.P Footwear
6217 SW Freeway
Houston, TX 77074
Phone#: 713-271-7463
http://www.wholesalecentral.com/fapfootwear

Fetpak Inc.
70 Austin Blvd.
Commack, NY 11725
Phone#: 800-88FETPAK
http://www.fetpak.com

Firstar International Trading
2334 S. Vineyard
Ontario, California 91761
Phone#: 909-923-0515
http://www.firstar.com

Forum Publishing Co.
383 East Main St.
Centerport, NY 11721
Phone#: 516-754-5000
http://www.forum123.com

Foot Log
P.O. Box 26683
Salt Lake City, UT 84120683
http://www.footlog.com

Foxy Lady Scents
P.O. Box 1387
Tulsa, OK 74101

Fresco's
3131 Candalaria NE #19
Albuquerque, NM 87107
Phone#: 505-889-3785
http://www.frescos.com

G Listings
A B C D E F G H I J K L M N O P Q R S T U V W X Y Z

Galaxy Electronics
1530 McDonald Ave
Brooklyn, NY 11230
Phone#: 800-221-8924

Garroe Surplus
405 Tarrytown Road Suite 372
White Plains, NY 10607
Phone#: 914-684-1455

Gary's Wholesale Inc.
30 West Main Street
Ashland, OH 44805

Gateway Information Group Inc.
1754 Technology Drive Ste #130
San Jose, CA 95110
Phone#: 408-453-6056

George Store
3597 Sparrow Rd.
Akron, OH 44333
Phone# 330-666-2226

Gibson Holders
3922 W 1 Ave
Eugene, OR 97402

Global Computer Supplies
11 Harbor Park Dr.
Port Washington, NY 11050
Phone#: 800-845-6225

Global Exports
5989 Braemar Place #105
Orlando, FL 32822
Phone#: 407-306-0718
http://www.bryceallen.com

Good N' Lucky Merchandise
PO Box 1185
Cheno Valley, AZ 86323

Good Sports Inc
1017 Sullivan Ave
S Windsor, CT 06074

GT & Associates
Phone#: 800-709-2682

Gutmann Cutlery Inc
120 S. Columbus Ave
Mt Vernon, NY 10553

H Listings
A B C D E F G H I J K L M N O P Q R S T U V W X Y Z

HarMatt Merchandising, Inc.
Phone#: 508-358-4250

Harmony Enterprises
Box 99
Harmony, ME 04942

Henry Textiles
819 S. Santee St. Suite 1102
Los Angeles, CA 90014
Phone#: 213-622-7980

H & J Liquidators
407 Domenic Court
Franklin Park, IL 60131
Phone#: 630-595-7717
http://www.surplus.net/hj

HMS Industries, Inc.
720 Fredrick Road
Baltimore, MD 21228
Phone#: 410-744-2200

Hobby Club
10 Hughes St. Suite A-102
Irvine, CA 92618
Phone#:714-461-0336
http://www.hobbyclub.com

Home Run Sports
970 St. Mary's Road
Winnipeg, Manitoba R2M 3R8
Phone#: 204-255-7687

Hoovers Wholesale Dist.
Food, beverage, tobacco
www.hoovers.com/industry/description

Honig's Whistle Stop
PO Box 1711
Ann Arbor, MI 48106
Phone#: 800-468-3284
http://www.honigs.com

Horn Sportswear
301 S. Cedar Ave
PO Box 525
So. Pittsburg, TN 37380-0525
Phone#: 888-471-5921

Hot Pockets
350 E. Tiogo Street
Philadelphia, PA 19134

Houseware Wharehouse, Inc.
112 Mango Tree Drive
Edgewater, FL 32132
Phone# 904-432-7848
Fax# 904-432-2599

I Listings
A B C D E F G H I J K L M N O P Q R S T U V W X Y Z

Import Wharehouse, Inc.
PO Box 29102
Dallas, TX 75229-0102
Phone#: 800-527-0102
http://www.wholesalewebdirect.com

India Craft Imports
230 E. Winston Street #44
Los Angeles, CA 90013

Phone#: 213-688-8785
http://www.wholesalewebdirect.com

Infomax Trading Corp.
450 Broome St.
New York, NY 10013-5906
http://www.closeoutusa.com

Integrity Plus
Phone#: 909-687-2952

Interchange Inc.
4820 Park Glen Road
Minneapolis, MN 55416
Phone#: 612-929-6669
http://www.interchangeinc.com

International Jewelry Traders Mfg., Inc.
2918 Gilroy St.
Los Angeles, CA 90039
Phone#: 323-953-9773

International Marketing
3927 NW North Rd.
Portland, OR 97229
Phone# 503-297-1338
http://www.surplus.net/aim-sales/

Intimate Apparel Connection
Phone#: 305-949-0925
http://www.intimate-apparel.com

Int'l Imports Inc.
5320 So. Penn. Ave
Oklahoma City, OK 73119-6005
Phone#: 405-681-8971
http://www.surplus.net/iiiinc

IPU
PO Box 9455
Elizabeth, NJ 07202

J Listings
A B C D E F G H I J K L M N O P Q R S T U V W X Y Z

Jacques Debois Perfumes
416 W. Huron
Ann Arbor, MI 48106

JAC of Trades
PO Box 3335
Laguna Hills, CA 92653

JAMO & Associates
1600 Wyatt Dr. Ste 4
Santa Clara, CA 95054
Phone#: 408-988-1169
http://www.jamo.com

JB Sirmans Imports
185 Ward St.
New Brunswick, NJ 08901

JHWhite Pubs Co.
PO Box 66471
Seattle, WA 98166
Phone#: 206-241-2682
http://www.aniota.com/~jwhite/

J & J Coin Jewelry
5451 Altona Dr.
Lexington, MI 48450

J & J Textile Co.
1313 Central Ave
Chattanooga, TN 37408
Phone#: 423-266-6340

Joissu Products Inc.
4627 LB McLeod Road
Orlando, FL 32811
Phone#: 800-233-8746
http://www.wholesalewebdirect.com

JRT Virginia
PO Box 1186
Mechanicsville, VA 23111-1186
Phone#: 804-228-3408

K Listings
<u>A</u> <u>B</u> <u>C</u> <u>D</u> <u>E</u> <u>F</u> <u>G</u> <u>H</u> <u>I</u> <u>J</u> <u>K</u> <u>L</u> <u>M</u> <u>N</u> <u>O</u> <u>P</u> <u>Q</u> <u>R</u> <u>S</u> <u>T</u> <u>U</u> <u>V</u> <u>W</u> <u>X</u> <u>Y</u> <u>Z</u>

King Of The Road Map Service
PO Box 55758
Seattle, WA 98155

KJ & M Distributor
PO Box 65
Fiskerville, RI 02823

Knox Concepts, Inc.
Phone#: 800-879-1373

Kodak Film Center
60 East 42nd Street
NY, NY 10165
Phone# 212-661-0752
Fax# 212-661-2767
http://www.filmcenter.com

Krafts By Kim
Route 2 Box 85A
Jasper, MO 64755

K & R Trading
761 S. Kirkman Rd
Orlando, FL 32811
Phone#: 407-521-0817

Kristie's Closeouts
Phone#: 877-991-0009
http://www.kristiesdeals.net

Kung-Ho International
PO Box 462003
Garland, TX 75046

L Listings
A B C D E F G H I J K L M N O P Q R S T U V W X Y Z

La Bell Time Inc.
Phone#: 305-940-1507

Lakeside Products Co.
6646 N. Western Ave
Chicago, IL 60645
Phone#: 773-761-5495
http://www.wholesalecentral.com/lakeside

Lasting Impressions
PO Box 22065
Lake Buena Vista, FL 32830

Lechler Labs Inc.
100 Red School House Rd
Chestnut Ridge, NY 10977

Leisure Craft
PO Box 45
Jamestown, RI 02835

Liquidation Mailing List
http://www.eis.net/list/

Liqui-Shield Services
2440 Sunbury Rd. Suite 102
Columbus, OH 43219
Phone#: 888-759-6022

Log Cabin Crafts
86 Ball Rd.
Townsend, MA 01469
Phone#: 508-597-5651
http://www.logcabintole.com

Logic Box Distribution
Phone#: 905-405-1541
http://www.logicbox.com

Lotions And Lace Co
2881 Hulen Place
Riverside, CA 92507

Lyben Computer Systems, Inc.
5545 Bridgewood
Sterling Heights, MI 48310
Phone#: 800-493-5777

M Listings

Macwarehouse
Dept. WBM97
PO Box 3013
Lakewood, NJ 08701-3013
Phone#: 800-255-6227
http://www.warehouse.com

Mansfield Advertising Agency
PO Box 837
Milltown, NJ 08850

Manufacturers Import Co
PO Box 33
Richmond, VA 23201

MAR.co
Phone#: 248-706-1500

Margolin Shoes Inc.
1935 S. Wabash
Chicago, IL 60616
Phone#: 312-225-5222
http://www.closeoutshoes.com

Mark Farmer
PO Box 9325

Knoxville, TN 37940
Phone#: 423-573-3814

Maxima Enterprises Inc.
Phone#: 905-709-1500

Mercantile Buyer's Service, Inc.
PO Box 090528
Milwaukee, WI 53209
Phone#: 800-752-7874
http://www.mercantilebuyers.com

Merchandise USA, Inc.
2221 S. Michigan Ave
Chicago, IL 60616
Phone#: 312-791-0070
http://www.merchandiseusa.com

Miami City Web
13235 SW 10 Terrace
Miami, FL 33184
Phone# 305-559-6279
Fax# 305-553-9509
http://www.gift-shop.com

Micro Direct
5326 Eagleswatch Court
Cincinnati, OH 45230
Phone#: 800-737-2447
http://www.microdirect.com

Mid-American Financial Group Inc.
333 W. North Ave Ste 347
Chicago, IL 60610
Phone#: 312-943-8850

Mid-Town Closeout
1103 South State Street
Salt Lake City, UT 84111
Phone#: 801-322-3085

Midwest Drug
619 ½ 8th Ste 5-9
PO Box 1447
Ft. Madison, IA 52632

Midwestern Co
4723 N. Pulaski Rd.
Chicago, IL 60630

MJH Enterprises
383 Westfield St.
Dedham, MA 02026
617-329-8506
http://www.expage.com/page/closeout

MTS Supply Co.
PO Box 188
Cedar Ridge, CA 95924
http://www.mtssupply.com

N Listings
A B C D E F G H I J K L M N O P Q R S T U V W X Y Z

Ness Trading Company/DBA Missouri Wheels
5730 Natural Bridge
St. Louis, MO 63120-1630
Phone#: 888-669-4335
http://www.mowheels.com

Network Express
933 S. Santa Fe Ave
Vista, CA 92084

New Directions Inc.
111 Fourth Ave, Suite 5F
NY, NY 10001

New Era Factory Outlet
20 Orchard St.
NY, NY 10002

New York Wholesale
660 Tidewater Dr. Ste H
Norfolk, VA 23504

Nippon Direct
14209 Garden Rd
Pearland, TX 77581
Phone#: 800-485-5050

Northwest Accounting Designs Inc.
330 SW 43rd St. Suite K311
Renton, WA 98390
Phone#: 206-862-8963
http://www.eskimo.com/~realtime

North Shore Distributors
1920 Scranton Road
Cleveland, OH 44113
Phone#: 216-696-6655

Novelty Liquidators
3521 W US 40
Greenfield, IN 46140
Phone#: 800-968-7442
http://www.wholesalecentral.com/novelty/

O Listings
A B C D E F G H I J K L M N O P Q R S T U V W X Y Z

Odyssey Jewelry
1920 Westminster Street
Providence, RI 02909
Phone#: 401-421-2230
http://www.wholesalecentral.com/odyssey

Old Colonial Anderson Mills
502-508 McAfee St.
Dalton, GA 30720

Omni Marketing International
PO Box 3323
Spokane, WA 99202
Phone#: 888-811-8864

Onelook Money Organizer
190 North Wiget Suite 220
Walnut Creek, CA 94598

Online Trading
Phone#: 905-565-0086
http://www.onlinetr.com

P Listings
A B C D E F G H I J K L M N O P Q R S T U V W X Y Z

Panam Pacific Group
37814 N. Cluny Ave.
Palmdale, CA 93550
Phone# 805-267-1525
http://www.salvage.com/panam/

Panwire LTD
1140 Broadway Suite 702
NY, NY 10031

Patrick Ferrell Imports
738 Design Ct. (303)
Chula Vista, CA 92911

PC Progress
1533 W. Lealand Ave
Chicago, IL 60640
Phone#: 773-506-6464
http://www.pcprogress.com

PD Enterprises
Main St.
PO Box 192006
San Francisco, CA 94119

Phelps Enterprises
2201 Faye Lane
Bakersfield, CA 93304-4903
Phone# 805-834-9261
Fax# 805-834-9261
http://www.formdec.com

Plus Size Outlet
Birmingham, AL
Phone#: 205-916-0144
http://www.plussizeoutlet.com

Plymouth Press
PO Box 2044
Miami, FL 33140

P.M. Belt Company
429 Marcy Ave
Brooklyn, NY 11206
Phone#: 800-762-3580
http://www.wholesalecentral.com/pmbelt

Popular Greeting Inc.
505 Blue Ball Road #140
Elkton, MD 21921
Phone# 800-505-5514
Fax# 410-392-3731
http://www.angelfire.com/biz/greetingcards/

Post Govt. Surplus
Phone# 503-658-4903

Premier Products Int'l
5302 56th Commerce Park Blvd
Tampa, FL 33610
Phone#: 800-231-0210
http://www.wholesalecentral.com/premierproducts

Premiere Publishers Inc.
Box 330309-Z
Ft. Worth, TX 76163

Promax International
Phone#: 305-412-0145

P.S. Intimates International
3288 N. Main St.
Stratford, CT 06497

Q Listings
A B C D E F G H I J K L M N O P Q R S T U V W X Y Z

Q Perfumes
1965 Tubeway Ave
Commerce, CA 90040
Phone#: 800-397-5221
http://www.wholesalewebdirect.com

R Listings
A B C D E F G H I J K L M N O P Q R S T U V W X Y Z

RAJ Plastics Inc.
16 Buhrstone Court
Owings Mill, MD 21117
Phone#: 410-654-3693
http://www.bagsonnet.com

Real Deals
8894 SW 129 Terrace
Miami, FL 33176
Phone#: 305-232-8260

Reid Sales
856 Wolverine Rd
Mason, MI 48854

Rhino Mart
11637 Los Nietos Road
Santa Fe Springs, CA 90670
Phone#: 562-699-1122
http://www.rhinomart.com

RJ's Discount Sales
3725 SW South Park Avenue
Topeka, KS 66609
Phone#: 877-855-0989
http://www.rjsks.com

R & K Video & Electronics
1135 Tower Road
Schaumburg, IL 60173
Phone#: 847-843-2981

Ronsonic Trading Corp
11 Jocama Blvd
Old Bridge, NJ 08857

Ross Trading Group
1 Rosemount Dr. #310
Scarboro, Ontario M1K 2W5 Canada
Phone#: 416-285-1980

Rothman & Assoc.
1862 Rollins Rd.
Burlingame, CA 94010
Phone# 514-697-3883

Royal Import Export Company
455 West First Street
Tustin, CA 92780
Phone#: 714-669-0593
http://www.royal-import-export.com

R & S Industries
8255-DS Brentwood Ind Dr.
St. Louis, MO 63144

RV Esquerra Company
9707 Harvard St. Unit 3
Bellflower, CA 90706

S Listings

A B C D E F G H I J K L M N O P Q R S T U V W X Y Z

Safeguard Technologies
2522 Hanover St.
Aurora, CO 80010

Salco International
1782 Calumet St.
Clearwater, FL 33765
Phone#: 727-466-9229
http://www.salconet.com

Sav-On
193 E. Highway M-35

Gwinn, MI 49841
Phone#: 906-346-7065
http://www.sav-on-closeouts.com

SavOn Closeouts
193 E. Hwy M-35
PO Box 1356
Gwinn, MI 49841
Phone#: 906-346-7065
http://www.wholesalewebdirect.com

Seb's Fashions, Inc.
PO Box 561744
Miami, FL 33156
Phone#: 305-278-7770

Sell-FREE
PO Box 22481
Alexandria, VA 22304
Phone#: 703-370-5468
http://www.sell-free.com

Sheely Wholesale Dist.
Everything for the jewelry trade
www.sheelywholesale.com/

Sheldon Cord Products
2201 W Devon Ave
Chicago, IL 60659
Phone#: 773-973-7070

Shiny Car
PO Box 2389
Mayaquez, PR 00681

Shoes & Boots
770 Worldwide Trading Inc.
Phone#: 718-369-2745

Shoe Trades Publishing
http://www.shoetrades.com

SIMCO
27231 Hwy Blvd
Katy, TX 77494
Phone#: 281-391-3912
http://www.simcoparts.com

S & K Liquidators
2067 Country Road E. West
New Brighton, MN 55112
Phone#: 612-628-9742
http://www.surplus.net/S&K/

Skateboard Directory
skateboarddirectory.com/pm/mp/c478447

Sky's Unlimited
4312 Walker Way
Sioux Falls, SD 57103

Slambamfun Merchandise
99 Gold St.
Brooklyn, NY 11201

S & M Distributors, Inc.
1211 SW 2nd Street
Pompano Beach, FL 33069
Phone#: 954-784-2854
http://www.smdistributors.com

Solomons Bargin Center
14255 Beach Blvd.
Jacksonville, FL 32250
Phone#: 904-233-0888
http://www.closeout.net/solomons

Southern Textile & California Clothes Outs
4119 N Freeway Blvd
Sacramento, CA 95834
Phone#: 916-485-3400
http://www.southerntextile.com

Special Gifts
PO Box 86487
Portland, OR 97286

Specialty Promotions
320 West 37th St.
5th Floor
NY, NY 10018

Spectrum Eagle
1500 Beverly Dr.
Clearwater, FL 34624

Spongex Corp.
6 Bridge St.
Shelton, CT 06484

Spotbuy
Phone#: 423-690-4229
http://www.spotbuy.com

SprayBottles Inc.
Phone#: 407-891-8624

SSH Corp.
PO Box 960071
Miami, FL 33296
Phone#: 407-679-5227

Star Merchandise
PO Box 3609
Thousand Oaks, CA 91359

Strawser Specialty Company
1318 S. Finley Rd
Dept 888D
Lombard, IL 60148

Sunbelt Wholesalers
11113 Harry Hines
Dallas, TX 75229

Sunland Imports
P.O. 37242
Tucson, AZ 85740
Phone# 520-531-0412
Fax# 415-697-3841

Sunshine Jewelry
PO Box 363
Kantishna River
Nenana, AK 99760

Sun Valley Emus, Inc.
Rte 1 Box 5A
Bryson, TX 76427
Phone#: 817-392-2225
http://www.jkinder.com

Surplus Asset Management
Phone#: 910-545-7720
http://www.surplus.net/sam

Surplus Direct
http://www.surplusdirect.com

Sweeney Stamps
841 S. 10th St.
Allentown, PA 18103

Syms Station
PO Box 2121
Peabody, MA 01960

Szco Supplies Inc.
PO Box 6353
Baltimore, MD 21230

T Listings
<u>A</u> <u>B</u> <u>C</u> <u>D</u> <u>E</u> <u>F</u> <u>G</u> <u>H</u> <u>I</u> <u>J</u> <u>K</u> <u>L</u> <u>M</u> <u>N</u> <u>O</u> <u>P</u> <u>Q</u> <u>R</u> <u>S</u> <u>T</u> <u>U</u> <u>V</u> <u>W</u> <u>X</u> Y Z

Target Music Distributors
7925 NW 66th St.
Miami, FL 33166

Terese LTD
Phone#: 706-878-2670

Textile Trading Associates
34-02C Review Avenue
Long Island City, NY 11101
Phone#: 718-786-1010

The Chip Merchant, Inc.
4870 Viewridge Ave
San Diego, CA 92123
Phone#: 800-808-2447 (#3)
http://www.thechipmerchant.com

The Closeout Net
http://www.closeout.net

The Clothing Club Inc.
5656 Broadway Ave
Cleveland, OH 44127
Phone#: 440-526-1861
http://www.theclothingclub.com

The Corner Cupboard
438 McGeorge Drive
Vinton, VA 24179
Phone#: 540-890-3148
http://www.angelfire.com/va/cornercupboard

The Discount Warehouse, Inc.
10092 NW 53 Street
Sunrise, FL 33351
Phone#: 954-746-8701
http://www.closeouts.digiscape.net

The Dog House
516 Jones Street
Dalton, FA 30742
Phone#: 706-226-7202

The Extra Mile
53 Pico Rd.
Clifton Park, NY 12065
Phone#: 800-560-2949
http://www.wholesalecentral.com/extramile/

The Leather Shop
RT 13 Box 984
Lake City, FL 32055

The Memory Store
13431 Montana Ave Ste F
Elpaso, TX 79938
Phone#: 800-989-4726

The Norchrist Group
2 Estate Dr.
Middletown, NY 10940
Phone#: 914-343-6536

The Panam Pacific Group
Phone#: 805-267-1525
http://www.salvage.com/panam

The Tor Company
6031 Rising Sun Ave
Philadelphia, PA 19111
Phone#: 215-342-8300
http://www.thetorcompany.com

The Zippo Store
1518 S. Karle
Westland, MI 48186
Phone#: 313-728-9722
http://www.thezippostore.com

Thomas Enterprises
Phone#: 201-501-0242

Thorson Guilds
Box 470886

Tulsa, OK 74147
http://www.wholesalecentral.com/spraybottles

Total Retails
300 Tower Lake
Edwardsville, IL 62025
Phone#: 618-659-4111

Trader Jack
460 Riggs Street NW
Salem, OR 97304
Phone#: 503-581-6654

Triple "T" Products, Inc.
PO Box 248
226 Chatham Street
Newport, NC 28570
Phone#: 252-223-2727

True Essence Inc.
12200-21 San Jose Blvd., Suite 176
Jacksonville, FL 32223
Phone#: 904-292-9057
http://www.wholesalewebdirect.com

T-Shirt Supply, Inc.
1352 N. Illinois Street
Indianapolis, IN 46202
Phone#: 317-634-4423

Two Harbors Outlet
1233 7th Ave

Two Harbors, MN 55616
Phone#: 218-834-4000

U Listings

<u>A</u> <u>B</u> <u>C</u> <u>D</u> <u>E</u> <u>F</u> <u>G</u> <u>H</u> <u>I</u> <u>J</u> <u>K</u> <u>L</u> <u>M</u> <u>N</u> <u>O</u> <u>P</u> Q <u>R</u> <u>S</u> <u>T</u> <u>U</u> <u>V</u> <u>W</u> X Y Z

Union Pharmacy
Phone#: 716-854-1205

Universal Badge Co.
169 O'Brien Hwy
Cambridge, MA 02141

Universal Liquidators
http://www.closeout.net/universal/

USA Bargains, Inc.
10096 NW 53rd Street
Ft. Lauderdale, FL 33351
Phone#: 954-962-2111

US Video, Inc.
1111 Rt 35
N. Ocean, NJ 07712
Phone#: 800-497-3637

V Listings
A B C D E F G H I J K L M N O P Q R S T U V W X Y Z

Valentini Distribution Centres
5520 Packard Road
Niagara Falls, NY 14304
Phone#: 716-804-0274

Volume Apparel Group
49 Rose Street
Stoughton, MA 02972
Phone#: 781-344-1400

W Listings
A B C D E F G H I J K L M N O P Q R S T U V W X Y Z

Warehouse One
9305 Cherokee Trail
Crossville, TN 38555
Phone#: 931-788-1011
http://www.warehouse-one.com

Warehouse Sales
25 Loring St.
Framingham, MA 01701
Phone#: 800-545-9438
http://www.warehousesales.com

Wholesale Imports
4101 Summer Ave
Memphis, TN 38122
Phone#: 800-222-4973
http://www.wholesalewebdirect.com

Wholesale World
2808 NW 112 Ave
Miami, FL 33172
Phone#: 305-418-4546
http://www.wwpcmac.com

Wholesale World, Inc.
7501 Harwin Dr. Suite D103
Houston, TX 77036
Phone#: 713-268-1688

William Johnson Auctioneers
PO Box 322
San Ganriel, CA 91778-0322
Phone#: 818-287-3827
http://www.dollarbill.com

W.L. Baumler Co
1744 Iowa Ave
Lorain, OH 44052
Phone#: 800-321-2501

Wig Wholesalers
Wigs, hairpieces, etc.

www.aaawigbiz.com/index-m-wholesale.htm

Worldwide Colors Inc.
153 Meachem Ave
Elmont, NY 11003

Worldwide Surplus Inc.
PO Box 69
Prairie, MS 39756
Phone#: 662-369-2747

Wolf Global Trading
220 Smith St.
Fort Collins, CO 80524
Phone#: 970-482-2421

Wuu Jau Co
801 Centennial Blvd
Edmond, OK 73013

XYZ Listings
A B C D E F G H I J K L M N O P Q R S T U V W X Y Z

X
X-Trade Co
5475 Repecho Drive, No K208
San Diego, CA 92124
Phone#: 619-569-1575

Y
Yes Man
http://www.yesman.com

Y & Y Imports
1365 Bennett Dr. #492
Longwood, FL 32750
Phone#: 407-332-9670

Z
Zebra Services
P.O. Box 520
Chester, VT 05143-0520

Please visit Donnylowy.com

0-595-27003-4

Printed in the United States
68800LVS00003B/143